Soft Skills at Work

Technology for Career Success

Beverly Amer

Northern Arizona University

COURSE TECHNOLOGY
CENGAGE Learning™

Australia • Brazil • Japan • Korea • Mexico • Singapore • Spain • United Kingdom • United States

COURSE TECHNOLOGY
CENGAGE Learning™

Soft Skills at Work: Technology for Career Success
Beverly Amer

Executive Editor: Marie L. Lee

Senior Product Manager: Kathy Finnegan

Product Manager: Erik Herman

Associate Acquisitions Editor: Brandi Henson

Associate Product Manager: Leigh Robbins

Editorial Assistant: Patrick Frank

Director of Marketing: Cheryl Costantini

Marketing Manager: Ryan DeGrote

Marketing Specialist: Jennifer Hankin

Developmental Editor: Fran Marino

Senior Content Project Manager:
  Jennifer Goguen McGrail

Composition: GEX Publishing Services

Art Director: Marissa Falco

Cover Designer: Marissa Falco

Copyeditor: Suzanne Huizenga

Proofreader: Green Pen QA

For product information and technology assistance, contact us at
Cengage Learning Customer & Sales Support, 1-800-354-9706

For permission to use material from this text or product, submit all requests online at **cengage.com/permissions**
Further permissions questions can be emailed to
permissionrequest@cengage.com

Some of the product names and company names used in this book have been used for identification purposes only and may be trademarks or registered trademarks of their respective manufacturers and sellers.

Any fictional data related to persons or companies or URLs used throughout this book is intended for instructional purposes only. At the time this book was printed, any such data was fictional and not belonging to any real persons or companies.

Course Technology, a part of Cengage Learning, reserves the right to revise this publication and make changes from time to time in its content without notice.

ISBN-13: 978-1-60334-014-4

ISBN-10: 1-60334-014-9

Course Technology
25 Thomson Place
Boston, MA 02210
USA

Cengage Learning is a leading provider of customized learning solutions with office locations around the globe, including Singapore, the United Kingdom, Australia, Mexico, Brazil, and Japan. Locate your local office at:
international.cengage.com/region

Cengage Learning products are represented in Canada by Nelson Education, Ltd.

For your lifelong learning solutions, visit **course.cengage.com**

Purchase any of our products at your local college store or at our preferred online store **www.ichapters.com**

Printed in Canada
1 2 3 4 5 6 7 12 11 10 09 08

Table of Contents

Preface

Thank you for adopting *Soft Skills at Work* for your students. This workbook is designed to help you prepare your students for the workplace by providing the chance to practice and apply career success principles to situations they will encounter. For the first time, you have the opportunity to provide your students practical and relevant life skills while continuing to develop their technical skills, all in one easy-to-use resource!

"Soft skills"—those defined as attitudes and behaviors that relate to critical thinking, problem solving, communication, collaboration, and presentation skills—not only help a student get a job in the career he or she aspires to, they are essential to long-term success in the workplace. A recent study conducted on behalf of The Association of American Colleges and Universities titled, *How Should Colleges Prepare Students To Succeed in Today's Global Economy?* reported that such skills are key areas of concern for employers around the world. How to gain and sharpen these skills will be explored in this book.

Further, an information technology workforce skills study prepared for Boston Area Advanced Technological Education Connections (BATEC) reports that certain technology skills taught by some schools and considered cornerstone achievements in career preparation by both students and faculty are "completely assumed" by business. In fact, in most cases, employers do not list technical proficiency in computer applications as a requirement for this reason.

The good news is that this book can help. What makes it different from anything else you may have seen is its unique combination of "reality" video episodes and a corresponding written workbook.

Soft skills are essential to long-term success in the workplace.

How to Use This Book

Soft Skills at Work combines an engaging workbook with video episodes on CD that help visually reinforce the content in the workbook chapters. Students should read the workbook material first, filling in the personal reflection spaces, before turning to the chapter's video episode to see the principles in action. As they watch the video clip, students should refer back to their workbook to analyze and critique the skills presented.

Using the written text and the video components together is essential for providing the maximum benefit to your students. Reading, observing, and then analyzing will help ensure that your students carry these principles out of your classroom and into the workplace.

At the end of each chapter, there is a Video Critique Worksheet to guide the analysis of the chapter's video episode. This worksheet is designed to help students critically evaluate what happened in the episode, as well as reflect on how they might have acted (or reacted) if they were in the same situation.

The end-of-chapter materials also include projects to reinforce or extend the knowledge gained from workbook readings. The projects include activities such as:

• Preparing a resume and cover letter

• Making a video of interviewing dos and don'ts

• Cleaning up your online persona

• Creating, analyzing, and correcting e-mail communications

• Researching collaboration software tools

• Preparing an effective team presentation

At a minimum, have students complete the video critique and one of the projects to give them a chance to practice critical thinking, communication, and problem solving skills. The results may not be pretty or perfect, but by offering them a safe environment to practice, they'll quickly learn and gain the confidence they need for future career success.

Upon completion of the workbook's activities, your students will be better equipped to enter the work force and start making their mark with confidence. Encourage them to keep the workbook and their work as part of their personal portfolios and resources that can be referred back to as needed throughout their careers.

Acknowledgements

This is my second project with Cengage Learning/Course Technology. The first one was *Computers in Our World, Second Edition,* which acquainted me with the incredibly detailed process of publishing textbooks. In the process of developing *Soft Skills at Work: Technology for Career Success*, I not only learned a great deal more about how good ideas become great products, but came to depend on a terrific team of publishing experts and colleagues who truly care about creating educational materials that make a difference in the lives of those who use them. At Cengage, Marie Lee, my editor, provided wonderful direction from the beginning and helped to shape the vision for the workbook and video series. Erik Herman and Fran Marino guided me through the operational details of making the ideas flow—on schedule!—and proved invaluable; offering suggestions and keeping me focused. Many others at Cengage, too numerous to mention, also made this project a priority and provided great skill in getting everything finished.

My colleagues at Northern Arizona University—T. S. Amer, Mary Bowers, David Albritton, and Brian Gregory—offered enthusiastic support for my ideas and gave generously of their time when I asked for it. From industry, Erika Sassaman of Grant Thornton LLP and Kaia Walton of KPMG LLP provided insights into the world of corporate recruiting and helped shape the materials included in the first two chapters. On the video production side, my editor, Bill Slater of Edit Alchemy, worked his magic in creating the finished video episodes that accompany this workbook, and was as excited as I was to see the finished segments get great reviews from students.

I must also acknowledge the many faculty members at colleges and universities across the nation who provided feedback about the project at conferences and Cengage events. Those of you who are forward-thinking and care about doing what's best for your students inspire me!

This book is dedicated to my parents, Thomas and Twila Elrod.

About the Author

Beverly Amer is on the faculty of the W. A. Franke College of Business at Northern Arizona University. She has taught computer information systems, management information systems, and accounting courses to thousands of students for nearly 15 years. In 2004-2005, she earned the Teacher of the Year award at the College. Prior to joining the faculty at Northern Arizona University, she was on the faculty of the University of Florida's Fisher School of Accounting, where she taught both accounting and information systems courses.

Her professional work experience includes several years with Andersen Consulting, where she worked on teams specializing in healthcare and public utility information systems development and installation. She also worked for many years in hospital administration positions before earning her MBA from The Ohio State University. She is a Certified Management Accountant (CMA), and has earned various Microsoft Office application certifications over the past few years.

Amer is also the author of *Computers in Our World, Second Edition,* and owns a media production company that specializes in creating real-world business case studies for the higher education market. Her passion is helping students connect their classroom learning experiences to the real world of business through the use of technology and media. When she's not working, she enjoys hiking, mountain biking, skiing, music, cooking, and exploring foreign countries that put her just beyond her comfort zone.

1 Career Preparation

Using Your Tech Skills for Career Preparation

Introduction

Most people enter college with the goal of graduating and securing a position in the career field they've dreamed of pursuing. If you are reading this book, chances are good that you're one of them. You are taking classes and learning methods, models, tools, and techniques that you can apply to real work situations down the road. These classes and their activities represent an investment in your future—one you are willing to make because you see the payoff ahead.

Yet there's more to landing that dream job than simply completing your coursework and earning good grades: You will need to interview for prospective jobs. And to do that, you must learn how best to prepare and present yourself. This requires combining the technical skills you're gaining in school with "soft skills." But, what exactly are soft skills? Starting with this chapter, you will find out. More important, you will come to realize that you won't stand a chance of succeeding in your chosen profession without them.

Objectives

In this chapter, you'll learn about the career preparation process and how you can apply technology skills to your advantage. This will help you gain an edge over the competition and build a solid base of knowledge to see you through your entire career. More specifically, you will learn:

- What a résumé does for you
- What a good résumé contains
- Whether you need a scannable or video résumé
- What a cover letter is for
- How to make a good first impression
- What to expect at the interview
- Why a thank-you note is a good idea

After reading the chapter, you'll get the chance to watch a short video of a typical day in a recruiter's life on campus, and critique the preparation and performance of the students being interviewed by using the information just learned in the chapter. You'll decide what they did right—and wrong—and what behaviors are worth copying.

KEY TERMS

chronological résumé
This résumé format organizes your qualifications by date, making it simple for the reader to follow your history, whether that history comprises time spent in school or working. This format is the most common one used by job seekers.

functional résumé
Résumé format in which your qualifications are structured into categories of skills that an employer might find desirable for an open position.

Finally, you'll be able to write down your own observations about your personal plans for career preparation and use the Web resources provided to learn more about résumés, interviews, and the job search process. Then you will apply your software skills to create a personalized cover letter, résumé, and thank-you note that you can use when your turn to interview finally arrives!

What a Résumé Does for You

Depending on the career path you've chosen, there may be great demand for workers with your skills. However, that demand does not automatically translate into an easy start on that path. Most job openings for professional positions require applicants to supply a current résumé that provides company recruiters with an initial picture of who you are, what experiences and education you've had, and the skills you bring to the company. What you write on your résumé determines whether you get a shot at an interview or end up in the circular file (aka the trash).

Your résumé is a written document that clearly presents your qualifications for a position along with your ability to use those qualifications for the benefit of the company. Its purpose is to compel the company's recruiter to meet you to determine how well you will fit in and whether you will add value to the enterprise. In a sense, it's your own personal sales brochure that tells potential employers why they need you on their team. As long as it is well written and you are qualified, you should get an interview.

> Where will you save your résumé, cover letter, and thank-you note documents for future use (USB drive, hard disk at home)? What will you name your files?
>
> _____
>
> _____
>
> _____
>
> _____

What a Good Résumé Contains

Most company recruiters spend less than 30 seconds scanning the résumés they get. This means your résumé must be organized, clear, and concise so the recruiter can easily size you up. You can format your résumé one of two ways: chronologically or functionally. A **chronological résumé** organizes your qualifications by date (see Exhibit 1-1). This makes it simple for the reader to follow your history—whether that history comprises time spent in school or working. This format is particularly useful when you have acquired experience over time in a series of positions and is the most common format used by job seekers, particularly those who are right out of college.

In a **functional résumé**, your qualifications are structured into categories of skills that the employer might find desirable for the open position (see Exhibit 1-2). Regardless of which format you choose, a good résumé will contain the following items:

Heading

Your name, address, telephone numbers, and e-mail address should all be included to make it easy for the company's recruiter to reach you. If you have a school address and a home address, it is fine to include both of them.

Most often, the heading is centered at the top of the page in a bold and larger font than the body of the résumé. If your school permits the use of your academic e-mail address for job correspondence, use it. Do not include a photograph of yourself unless your appearance is a bona fide job requirement. And avoid inappropriate and unprofessional e-mail addresses that are quirky or juvenile, such as "partyboy7" or "babyshuga." Think about what such addresses would say to a potential employer about your personality and professionalism.

Jill Tanner
15066 McConnell Circle
Reno, Nevada 89509
(775) 555-1445
jtanner@ureno.edu

OBJECTIVE
Entry-level investment analyst position in a regional or national financial investment company.

Qualifications

Team leadership experience	Financial analysis skills	Detail-oriented work ethic
Ability to translate financial language into terms clients understand	Creative and skilled writer	Ability to develop detailed plans and meet deadlines

Work Experience
e-Vestments, real estate investment company, *customer service representative,* May 2006--present
- Developed schedule for regular review of small (less than $100,000) client portfolios
- Created standard PowerPoint presentation on investing basics for employees speaking at local service club luncheons, such as Rotary and Kiwanis
- Researched investment options for clients
- Analyzed investment portfolio performance for clients with net worth up to $1 million
- Wrote company's quarterly investor newsletter to generate interest in company's real estate investment services

Small Business Administration, *volunteer business analyst,* October 2007--August 2008
- Prepared financial statements and business plans for clients seeking SBA loans
- Coordinated teams of volunteer business analysts while working part-time at the Small Business Administration

Education
University of Reno, Reno, Nevada
    B.S., Business (Finance), December 2008
    Overall GPA: 3.52/4.00
    Courses include: Investing for Individuals, Real Estate Finance and Investment, Financial Analysis and Working Capital Management, Corporate Financial Management, Financial Statement Analysis

Extra-Curricular Activities, Certifications, and Awards
- Team Captain, University of Reno women's golf team, August 2008--present
- Microsoft Certified Application Specialist, Excel 2007, May 2008
- Women's Athlete of the Year, Sierra region, May 2008

References
Available upon request

Exhibit 1-1 Chronological Résumé Example

What type of résumé format do you think would work best for you? Write down what your heading will contain.

_____

_____

_____

_____

Jill Tanner
15066 McConnell Circle
Reno, Nevada 89509
(775) 555-1445
jtanner@ureno.edu

OBJECTIVE
To obtain an entry-level investment analyst position in a regional or national financial investment company.

EXPERIENCE
• Researched investment options, including exchange-traded funds, for student team projects and clients
• Analyzed investment portfolio performance for clients with net worth up to $1 million
• Wrote company's quarterly investor newsletter to generate interest in company's financial services

ORGANIZATIONAL
• Maintained detailed spreadsheets linked to the Web with stock portfolio investment performance data
• Coordinated teams of volunteer business analysts while working part-time as the Small Business Administration

PLANNING
• Developed schedule for regular review of small (less than $100,000) client investment portfolios
• Created standard PowerPoint presentation on investing basics for employees speaking at local service club luncheons, such as Rotary and Kiwanis
• Prepared financial statements and business plans for clients seeking SBA loans

EMPLOYMENT
May 2006–present, e-Vestments, real estate investment firm, *customer service representative*
October 2007–August 2008, Small Business Administration, *volunteer business analyst*

SKILLS
•   Strong customer service orientation
•   Detail-oriented
•   Inquisitive and analytical acumen
•   Advanced Excel 2007 skills (Microsoft Certified Application Specialist, May 2008)

EDUCATION
University of Reno, Reno, Nevada
        B.S., Business (Finance), December 2008
Overall GPA: 3.52/4.00

Exhibit 1-2 Functional Résumé Example

Objective

Usually no more than one or two sentences, your objective gives the potential employer an idea of the type of job you are seeking. Consider the following objective statement for someone applying for an entry-level systems analyst position:

Objective: To obtain a position as an entry-level systems analyst in an international management consulting company.

This objective plainly tells the reader what position this person is seeking, the job level, and the type of company he or she wants to work for.

Avoid using phrases such as "growth opportunity" or "challenging position" as these are generally regarded as too vague to be meaningful. You can make your objective even more compelling by personalizing it for the company you are applying to. For example:

Objective: To obtain a position as an entry-level systems analyst at Encore Consulting, Inc.

> Write your objective statement here.
>
> _____
> _____
> _____
> _____

Qualifications

This section briefly describes your experience and the kinds of skills you offer the company. A bulleted list is most effective in organizing your qualifications for easy reading. There is no need to be verbose here. You will have the opportunity to explain your experience and skills in greater detail in the next section. Exhibit 1-1 gives examples of some qualifications in the table.

> What qualifications best describe you?
>
> _____
> _____
> _____
> _____

Section Headings

Whether you use the chronological or functional résumé format, section headings will provide a logical structure to the body of your résumé. In a chronological résumé, the section headings might consist of *Education*, *Work Experience*, *Organizations*, or *Volunteer and Community Service*. In your *Education* section, be sure to spell your school names correctly and fully, with city and state information. Most recruiters like to see a grade point average (GPA) included, whether it's your overall GPA or the GPA in your major courses. Indicate the scale used, such as a 3.42/4.0 scale.

In a functional résumé, the section headings might be *Systems Analysis*, *Programming*, *Consulting*, *Project Management*, or other descriptive titles. The skills and experiences you list in these functional areas should be broad enough so that the recruiter can easily see how they would be relevant for the open position as well as the future needs of the organization.

> Which résumé format is best for you? List the section headings that best fit your background and experience.
>
> _____
> _____
> _____
> _____

Descriptions

This is where the employer will see your accomplishments and successes. You want to convey that if you were able to achieve great things in the past, you also will do so in the future. The keywords you choose can help demonstrate your ability. Underneath each heading, describe your experience and skills using action verbs. For example, words such as "managed," "organized," "planned," and "wrote" are strong and active. If you supervised employees or managed financial resources, say so. If you identified a problem and came up with the solution, describe it. Emphasize what you accomplished and why this was of value to your employer.

Avoid phrases such as "Duties included" or "Responsibilities were" as they are weak and ineffective in conveying the nature of your experience. For example, if you worked at the drive-thru window of a fast-food restaurant, you might say, "Managed the accuracy and delivery of drive-thru orders for (name of restaurant) with a team of three employees. Consistently met customer service order delivery targets of 90 seconds or less and handled 65% of total lunchtime business for the restaurant." This is preferable to stating that your responsibilities included order taking, cash handling, and food delivery.

What action verbs describe what you have done?

_____

_____

_____

_____

Other Skills and Qualifications

This last section provides a place to list items that don't neatly fit into other categories. For example, your ability to speak Spanish fluently goes here, along with your membership in professional organizations, publications you've contributed to, and honors or certifications you've earned. It's fine to include accomplishments that are not directly job-related that could help you stand out, such as being a finalist on a TV game show, qualifying for the Olympics, or organizing a charity fund-raising event for the local animal shelter.

References

You must provide the names and contact information for several individuals who can speak to your personal and professional qualifications, if asked. However, they should not be listed on your résumé; it's sufficient to state "References available upon request." But those references should be printed out and ready to deliver when this request is made, whether at the interview or later. Be sure you approach your potential references ahead of time to get their permission. Let them know your plans for seeking a position so they are not caught off-guard when the company calls to get their input on your qualifications.

List the names, addresses, and phone numbers of at least three people who could serve as references for you.

_____

_____

_____

_____

The most common mistakes people make on résumés range from grammatical errors to outright fabrication of qualifications. Sometimes job applicants provide false or misleading information hoping it will help them secure the desired job. But this is a dangerous path to take, according to a survey of hiring managers conducted by CareerBuilder.com. The survey found that 57% of hiring managers have found a lie on a candidate's application, even though only 5% of applicants admit to such falsifications. In nearly all cases, the applicant did not get hired as a result of falsifying his or her résumé.

Obviously, you don't want to damage your chances of securing that coveted career position. Some mistakes to avoid include:

- Typos, inaccuracies, and lies
- Poor or no formatting—small or mixed fonts (smaller than size 10), odd margins
- Chunky paragraphs that are hard to read
- Inappropriate content—from e-mail and Web addresses to irrelevant jobs and experiences
- Too much creativity—cute graphics, scented or funny-textured paper, or other over-the-top means of standing out from the crowd
- Lack of focus, or no clear objective or reason for applying for the specific job opening

> As you write your résumé, check off each item on this list to be sure you've thought through each one.
>
> _____
>
> _____
>
> _____
>
> _____

Scannable and Video Résumés

Some companies rely on scanning software to pre-screen job applicants. These programs rely on keyword filters, usually nouns that the company has identified as relevant to its needs. If you send your résumé to a company that uses such software, your document should contain keywords from the position announcement to help you pass the initial scan. However, don't fabricate or overstate your qualifications because a human reviewer eventually will read your résumé and can see through such attempts to fool the software.

Video résumés are another matter altogether. For the on-campus recruitment process, the video résumé is unnecessary. However, online job posting sites do accept such files; and in some industries, such as theatre or the arts, they can be an effective way of visually presenting your qualifications and portfolio. Do some research before embarking on such a venture because a cheesy or amateurish video résumé can backfire and might even end up on YouTube as an example of what _not_ to do!

> Which companies you are interested in working for require or accept these résumé formats?
>
> _____
>
> _____
>
> _____
>
> _____

What Employers Say

Regardless of the position you seek, most employers are looking to hire candidates who demonstrate the ability to think analytically and apply quantitative problem-solving skills to the tasks at hand. Strong oral and written communication skills are important as well, along with the ability to work with—and lead—others in accomplishing work tasks. We'll address each of these skill sets in later chapters. But if you can strengthen your résumé by listing your abilities in these areas, be sure to include them.

> What strengths do you have in the above noted areas?
>
> _____
> _____
> _____
> _____

The Cover Letter

With your résumé complete, it's time to write your cover letter. Think of the cover letter as a summary of your interests and qualifications. This is your first chance to sell yourself and hook the reader so he or she will want to meet you. The contents must be perfect—no typos or strange phrases that you wouldn't use in real life. An example of a cover letter is shown in Exhibit 1-3.

One of the most common mistakes people make on their cover letters is not addressing the letter to anyone in particular. A letter addressed "Dear Sir or Madam" or "To Whom It May Concern" tells the reader you didn't care enough to find out who would be reviewing your correspondence. That's not the first impression you want to make! So do a little digging and find out who the human resources director is, or the name of the person doing the hiring.

In the opening sentence, indicate the position you are applying for and where you learned about it. Then provide some indication that you have reviewed the qualifications and believe you are the right person for the position.

> Write a sample opening sentence for your cover letter here.
>
> _____
> _____
> _____
> _____

In the body of the letter, summarize your qualifications—a bulleted list works well for this—to make it easy for the reader to see why you might be a good fit for the position. By doing a good job here, the reader will want to turn the page and review the details of your résumé and contact you for an interview. That's your goal!

> List your key qualifications here.
>
> _____
> _____
> _____
> _____

Jill Tanner
15066 McConnell Circle
Reno, Nevada 89509
(775) 555-1445
jtanner@ureno.edu

September 15, 2008

Mr. Ben Shuman
Manager, Human Resources
Paramount Investment Corp.
45 South Virginia Lane
Reno, Nevada 89519

Dear Mr. Shuman:

I am applying for the investment analyst position that was advertised this week in the placement office at the University of Reno. Based upon my education and background, I believe I am a good fit for this position.

The position announcement indicates you are seeking a team player with excellent analytical, oral, and written communication skills, and a B. S. degree in Business, with an emphasis in Accounting or Finance. I plan to graduate in December with a B. S. degree in Finance from the University of Reno. Some of my relevant coursework is shown in the table, below. In addition, I have held a part-time job as a customer service representative with e-Vestments, a local investment company specializing in real estate ventures, for the past two years and found this position ideal for honing my understanding of financial markets and investments.

Course	Skills
Investing for Individuals	Researching personal investment strategies, analyzing personal retirement portfolios to balance risk and return
Financial Analysis and Working Capital Management	Analyzing pro-forma financial statements for decision making, managing assets for small businesses
Real Estate Finance and Investment	Applying principles of rate of return, taxation, appraisal, and financing options to real estate investments

I'm confident I have the requisite skills and background to make a contribution to your company's success, and am excited about the prospect of using my education and experience to the benefit of Paramount Investment Corp.

If you think I'm the candidate you are seeking to fill this position, or would like more information, you may reach me at (775) 555-1445 or via e-mail at jtanner@ureno.edu. Thank you for your consideration.

Sincerely,
(Signature)

Jill Tanner

Exhibit 1-3 Cover Letter Example

At the end, you can also indicate that you will follow up in a short period of time—say, a week or so—to schedule an interview. Don't be shy about calling if you really want the job. Most employers value applicants who follow up, even if there are no job openings. But be careful—calling more than once a week can be annoying and may disqualify you from the running when there is an opening in the future. And don't have a parent do the follow-up for you. That's a sure sign that you are not yet ready for a professional career.

Finally, close the letter by thanking the reader for considering you for an interview and sign your name.

Making a Good First Impression

You are probably familiar with the phrase, "a picture is worth a thousand words." The theory that underlies this statement also applies to you and your appearance. That's because how you look is the picture you present to the world every day. When it comes to preparing for your job search and interviews, the image presented by your résumé is only part of your picture. The rest comes into play when you meet the company's representative, face-to-face, at the interview.

To complicate matters, when you do get that important in-person interview, you only have a few minutes to make a good first impression, according to some studies. So getting your appearance right is critical if the picture you want to present is an accurate reflection of who you are. Hiring managers are not shy about revealing what makes an impression—good or bad. "A suit jacket and tie are essential for men," says one major corporate recruiter from the Southwest. "That first impression tells me how serious you are about working for my company." Another recruiter adds, the applicant should "Look me in the eye and shake my hand with a smile. This is a great way to start off the interview."

The guidelines given here are not set in stone. For example, if you are applying for a creative position where nobody dresses in suits, then a more casual approach to interview attire is fine. Do some research ahead of time so you don't make the wrong impression at the interview. Call the human resources department of the company or seek advice from the career counselors at your school if you're not sure. Often, the attire worn to the interview is expected to be more formal even if the workplace is casual. Your goal is to underscore your competence and professionalism by your appearance. It's better to be over-dressed and taken seriously than to be disqualified for the position because of your appearance.

If you think these guidelines are too picky, remember that the job market is competitive. If you don't follow the guidelines, others still will. You will make the recruiter's job of eliminating you as a candidate much easier if you don't pay attention to the impression you make.

What type of dress code does your chosen career have? How does that translate into what you should wear to the interview?

_____

_____

_____

_____

Impression #1: Attire
Men:

- Clean suit, shirt, and silk tie in a conservative pattern (no jeans or casual sweaters or ties with questionable graphics or sports team logos)
- Belt that coordinates with suit (black belt with black or gray suit, for example)
- Socks that match your pants (not white)
- Dress shoes—polished with heels that are not worn down (no sport shoes, white socks, or athletic gear)

Women:

- Clean suit—skirts no shorter than an inch above the knee; depending on the job, nice slacks (never jeans) may be OK if common for the industry
- Blouse that is not too low cut or gaps open at the buttons when you move (bend over and stretch your arms back to test)
- Neutral undergarments and hosiery—no patterns or holes

- Heels 2 ½ inches high or less, closed toe and heel to match outfit; no strappy evening wear
- Conservative make-up with neutral colors—save the bright blue, green, and sparkles for evening

Both:

- Pressed and clean clothing; no stains, tears, patches, or missing buttons
- Empty pockets to avoid bulges or jingling change or keys (put all of this in your briefcase)
- No lace, ruffles, or shiny fabrics
- Avoid clingy knits or anything too revealing or low cut
- Colors—black, gray, navy (solid color or subtle stripe OK)
- Briefcase or portfolio instead of backpack and purse, with items discussed below
- No flip-flops or casual sandals

Impression #2: Appearance & Grooming

- Shower, use deodorant, and brush your teeth the day of the interview; consider using breath mints right before the interview and brushing your teeth if you had garlic or other strong flavors for lunch
- No colognes or perfumes, as some people are allergic
- Smokers—minimize exposure to smoke prior to the interview so you don't carry a cloud with you into the room
- No chewing gum, candy, or tobacco products
- Neat haircut, not over-styled; natural color (not purple, pink, or green)
- Freshly shaved face for men—moustaches and beards are sometimes considered negative for new employees, but check your industry
- Cover tattoos and remove piercings (especially tongue, lip, nose, eyebrow); earrings are OK for women but not more than one per ear
- Fingernails clean and hands scrubbed; natural nails, clear polish, or French manicure for women—no piercings or appliqués
- Remove excessive jewelry—leave the flashy jewelry at home; men: dress watch, wedding or class ring only, no earrings; women: dress watch, necklace, and one pair of earrings to coordinate with outfit; no sport watches, only one ring per hand

Impression #3: Technology

- Turn off your cell phone during the interview; wait until you are out of the building to make calls or send text messages
- Change the music callers hear to something non-offensive while waiting to connect or leave a message on your cell phone
- Leave the MP3 player and earphones in your briefcase, in your car, or at home

> Make this list your personal interview checklist. Which of these tips did you not know before reading this section?
> _____
> _____
> _____
> _____

KEY TERMS

mock interview
A practice interview that helps prepare candidates for the real thing and provides valuable feedback on their strengths and weaknesses.

behavioral interviewing
Involves asking candidates about how they reacted or handled situations or events in their background.

The Interview

Congratulations! Your résumé got you an interview, but it won't get you the job. You need to spend some time preparing for the interview.

If you haven't already researched the company, you should do so now. The Internet makes it easy to do basic research. At a minimum, use a search engine such as Google to locate the company's official Web site. Read about its products and services, locations, and press releases. Review the posted financial information for investors to gain a sense of size and markets. That basic accounting class you had will come in handy here. Then expand your search to other online news articles: who are the company's competitors, what effect is the economy having on the industry, what is the company's growth potential?

> What resources are available to you for doing basic company research?
> _____
> _____
> _____
> _____

Next, practice your responses to interview questions. Ask your school's placement office for some examples. Or locate some sample sets on the Web by conducting a search for "job interview questions." You won't be asked all these questions, but you must be prepared to respond quickly, succinctly, and honestly to any question you are asked. Participate in **mock interviews** at your school. A mock interview is an interview conducted for practice. Recruiters say this always helps to prepare candidates for the real thing since you get a chance to practice without penalty, and receive valuable feedback on your strengths and weaknesses.

As you scan the interview questions you collected, you might note that some of them ask for descriptive information, such as "Tell me what you did at Job X last summer." Others are more situation-based. This is a type of interview technique called **behavioral interviewing**, which involves asking candidates about how they reacted or handled situations or events in their background. This is the preferred approach on college campuses today. In this case, the interviewer wants to hear how you behaved in a particular situation. For example, if the interviewer asks how you handled an angry customer, he or she wants to see how you might respond when such a situation arises in the future. Be prepared to answer questions about how you identified a problem, developed solutions, selected the best one, and implemented that choice. At a minimum, you can expect to be asked about a time when you led a team.

> Some sample behavioral interview questions found online include:
> _____
> _____
> _____
> _____

Some Tips for the Big Day

- When you go to the interview, be sure to show up five to ten minutes early. Allow yourself plenty of time to get to the interview location, park, and locate the office. Bring a small briefcase or folio containing a couple pens, a pad of paper, extra copies of your résumé, and a few copies of your reference list, in case the interviewer requests them. If a portfolio of work projects is essential to the interview, make sure the folio and the work inside are organized, clean, and neat.

- Turn off your cell phone—even a vibrating phone can be heard—and leave the MP3 player and earphones at home, in your briefcase, or in your car.
- When you meet the interviewer, stand up straight, smile, look the person in the eye, and extend your right hand to shake the person's hand. A quick but firm shake is all that is required. No need to pump your arm or squeeze the person's hand too hard.
- When you sit down, place your briefcase or portfolio next to you on the floor. Place your hands in your lap; and if you must cross your legs, do so at the ankle. Avoid swinging crossed legs while seated to minimize distraction.
- Be sure to have two or three questions prepared to ask the interviewer—something about the company you discovered in your research, questions about the company's employee performance review process or telecommuting policies, or a comment about a recent news event that affects the company. Keep it upbeat yet demonstrate that you have done your homework. If you don't have any questions, the message you send to the recruiter is that you really aren't that interested in the job.

What are some good questions to ask at the end of an interview?

_____

_____

_____

_____

- As the interviewer signals the end of the interview, stand up and shake the interviewer's hand again. It's acceptable to ask about the next steps in the interview process and when you can expect to hear back from the company about the position. Also be sure to thank the interviewer for his or her time.

The Thank-You Note

The interview is over; you did everything correctly. The job should be yours, right? Not so fast. You still have one more task to complete—a thank-you note. Whether it's typed or handwritten, a note sent to the interviewer within 24 hours of the interview helps to round out the great first impression you made in person. It demonstrates that you know more about business relationships and communication than what's written on the résumé, and that you are serious about wanting the job. If more than one person interviewed you, then send each one a note.

According to Katherine Hansen at QuintCareers.com, only about 5% of people seeking jobs follow up with a thank-you note after the interview. Do you see the opportunity to set yourself apart here? If the company culture is more formal, send a typed note. If it's more casual, or you had a special rapport with the interviewer, consider sending a handwritten note. A sample thank-you note is included in Exhibit 1-4. Be sure to personalize your thank-you by commenting on something the interviewer said that was meaningful to you, for example. And, just like your résumé and cover letter, be sure to proofread it so it's free of typos and grammatical errors. After all, this is one more chance to sell yourself and help seal the deal.

What about an e-mail thank you? There are mixed feelings among company recruiters on this point. If the company culture relies heavily on e-mail for communication—and you've been corresponding with the company in this fashion already—then a quick e-mail message might be fine. But be sure to also follow up with a paper note. Do not send a text message. There are plenty of good thank-you note examples online. So if the one in Exhibit 1-4 doesn't quite work for you, take a look at some online samples to help craft one that better suits your style.

October 1, 2008

Jill Tanner
15066 McConnell Circle
Reno, Nevada 89509
(775) 555-1445
jtanner@ureno.edu

Mr. Ben Shuman
Manager, Human Resources
Paramount Investment Corp.
45 South Virginia Lane
Reno, Nevada 89519

Dear Mr. Shuman:

Thank you for meeting with me last week to discuss the career opportunities at your firm. As we discussed, my educational background and work experience seem to be a good fit for the entry-level investment analyst position at Paramount Investment Corp., and I look forward to being able to contribute to the company's future success.

As mentioned in the interview, I can bring a fresh perspective to your work environment from my recent experience as a business analyst at the Small Business Administration. Working with potential new small business owners has really given me a good understanding of how important solid investment research and advice can be to clients as they build their businesses. I'm also looking forward to applying the knowledge gained in my college coursework to real client situations and helping them realize their financial goals.

I appreciate the time you took to meet with me today. I remain very interested in working for you and look forward to hearing from you soon about this position.

Sincerely,

(Signature)

Jill Tanner

Exhibit 1-4 Sample Thank-You Note

Reasons People Don't Get Job Offers

Aside from not following the advice provided in this workbook, there are other reasons people don't get hired. As you look over Exhibit 1-5, you'll see that some of them are pretty obvious but others are more subtle. Use this list to make sure you avoid mistakes.

Poor personal hygiene or appearance	Negative attitude about past employers or work assignments	Lack of genuine interest in employer
Overly aggressive or arrogant	Lack of enthusiasm, confidence, or poise	No eye contact
Late for interview	More interested in money than position	Unwilling to start at the bottom
Unrealistic salary or benefits expectations	Carelessness on résumé and other correspondence	Failure to ask questions during the interview
Lack of tact, maturity, or courtesy	No sense of humor	Inability to answer questions clearly

Exhibit 1-5 Common Reasons People Don't Get Job Offers

Wrap-up

It might seem like a lot of work to prepare for—and land—the job you really want. But as you learned in this chapter, using your word processing and Web search skills can help the preparation go more smoothly. Use this checklist to assess your own preparedness. If something is missing, now is the time to correct it.

	Checklist—Before & After the Interview
❑	Résumé written and sent or posted
❑	Cover letter written and sent with résumé, as needed
❑	Company research done before interviews
❑	Interview questions researched and responses practiced
❑	Interview clothing selected, cleaned, and pressed; shoes polished and briefcase prepared with needed items
❑	Day planner updated with interview appointments
❑	Thank-you notes written and sent
❑	Follow up with companies within two weeks to express interest—82% of companies expect to be contacted, according to a Robert Half International survey

Tech Skills and Web Resources

Tech Skills
This chapter has introduced you to:

- The use of installed and online Word 2007 templates
- The use of a search engine to research careers, employers, and interview preparation

Web Resources
Perform a Google search for "university career services." If your own school doesn't have resources available, check out one of the schools Google returns in your search. A few notable ones are listed here:

Johns Hopkins University Career Management Program:
http://hrnt.jhu.edu/cmp/

Virginia Tech Career Services:
www.career.vt.edu/JOBSEARC/Resumes/purpose.htm

More information on resumes:
www.careerjournal.com/jobhunting/resumes/20070101-ransom.html
www.monster.com
http://jobsearch.about.com/od/resumes/a/aa040801a.htm

More information on dressing for the interview:
http://jobsearch.about.com/od/interviewsnetworking/a/dressforsuccess.htm

More information on Careers:
The Bureau of Labor Statistics Occupational Outlook Handbook
www.bls.gov/oco/
www.thecareerproject.org/
http://online.wsj.com/careers

Projects

Video Briefing

The first video episode introduces you to a company called Encore. Encore is a professional services firm, which means it provides consulting services to other businesses. The firm's services range from providing information systems solutions to providing strategic business planning and management consulting. Encore typically hires a small number of college students right after graduation to work as consultants on teams. Corporate recruiter Candace Johnson is on campus to interview several students for positions with the firm.

As you watch the video, use the Video Critique Worksheet that follows this section to analyze the preparation and performance of the students who are interviewing for consulting positions with Encore. Then use your analysis to determine how you would have prepared if you were interviewing with the company.

Video Critique Worksheet

Watch the Chapter 1 video, "The Interview." Based on what you learned in this chapter, critique each student's preparation.

1. Matthew Brady
Things done well:

_____
_____

Where he went wrong:

_____
_____

Do you think a job will be offered? Why or why not?

_____
_____
_____

2. Jill Tanner
Things done well:

_____
_____

Where she went wrong:

_____
_____

Do you think a job will be offered? Why or why not?

_____
_____
_____

3. Sophie Aguilar
Things done well:

_____
_____
_____

Where she went wrong:

_____
_____

Do you think a job will be offered? Why or why not?

_____
_____

What specific actions will you take to prepare for your own job search and interviews?

_____
_____
_____

What would you have done differently if you were interviewing for a position with Encore?

_____
_____
_____

What mistakes might you have made if you hadn't read this chapter and watched the video?

_____
_____

Writing a Winning Résumé, Cover Letter, and Thank-You Note

Writing Your Personal Résumé

Using the information and Web resources from this chapter, prepare your personal résumé, a cover letter, and a thank-you note. If desired, you may use one of the templates provided in Word 2007 to help you format each item. To find them, click the Microsoft Office Button and then click New. In the New Document window, click Installed Templates. Select the one you want and click Create. You may also download templates online—the list for different types, including letters and résumés, is shown under the Microsoft Office Online heading.

Which Word 2007 template, if any, do you plan to use?

_____

_____

_____

_____

What personal information do you need to gather: job history, volunteer work, school activities? List it here. Go back through the workbook notes you took and use them to create your résumé.

_____

_____

_____

_____

Don't worry if you don't have many entries in each category; you can add to the résumé as you gain experience over time. Be sure you give your résumé a meaningful name and store it where you can retrieve it later.

Career Research

Investigating Online and Local Career Resources

There are many career resources available online at Web sites such as http://online.wsj.com/careers and www.monster.com. Career services might be available at your school as well—through an advising center or a career placement office. If you haven't yet investigated the online resources, now is the time to try them out. And if you have never set foot inside your school's career center, then make time to stop in and learn about the assistance available. Ask about sample résumés, mock interviews, and other services they provide.

In this assignment, write a brief summary of the online resources you located for your chosen career. What did they offer?

_____

_____

_____

_____

What do you think will be most useful to you in the future?

_____

_____

_____

_____

In addition to the information gathered for online resources, add a few paragraphs to your summary about your school's resources. For example, at your school's career center, what services are offered?

_____

_____

_____

_____

What steps should you be taking now to be ready for interviews when the time comes?

_____

_____

_____

_____

Think You Can Do Better?

Making a Video Demo of Interview Dos and Don'ts

You've watched the video episode featuring Matthew, Jill, and Sophie going through the interview process. Think you can do better? Then grab your video camera and make your own video, demonstrating both the right and wrong ways to prepare or dress. Get creative here—your instructor may have you work in teams or submit the video for use by your school's placement office, or you may find that YouTube is the outlet of choice for presenting your take on career preparation and interviewing.

2 Your Online Persona

Introduction

The information you choose to convey to the world about yourself during a job search is no longer limited to what's included on your résumé. What you voluntarily post about yourself on the Internet—part of your **online persona**—is a natural extension of the image you present to the public.

Ranked among the top Web sites people visit regularly, social networks such as MySpace and Facebook have become some of the Internet's fastest-growing entities. Starting from nothing in 2003, they have become the daily points of connection, communication, and community for millions of people around the world. Personal data, photos, videos, messages, and more fill personal pages as people document their lives online. Blogs and wikis also have found a home as more people choose to digitally express themselves on the Internet.

With around-the-clock access to this personal information, questions related to both appropriateness and privacy have started to surface. Although you might post photos and comments online to keep your friends and family informed, companies have used these same postings as a rich source of information to give them a more complete picture of who you really are and how you are likely to behave as an employee. The line between what is considered private information and what is considered fair game by employers has become blurred. Knowing how to best manage your online persona has never been more important or relevant.

Objectives

In this chapter, you will:

- Learn about the role social networks play in a working professional's life
- Discover what types of content are acceptable for posting to blogs and wikis, and what to avoid
- Explore the diminishing realm of personal privacy and the growing concerns over information security

Social Networks, Blogs, Wiki Postings, and Your Career

KEY TERMS

social network
A Web site that allows individuals to connect with others. Users can post photo, video, audio, and text content about themselves on custom-created digital pages, and then create a network of friends linked through other people's personal pages.

blog
An online journal, usually written in chronological order by an individual.

wiki
A collaborative Web site that permits users to edit or add content to the site.

With the rapid growth of social networks on the Internet, the line between your personal life and public life is sometimes difficult to distinguish. A **social network** is a Web site that allows individuals to connect with others. Users can post photo, video, audio, and text content about themselves on custom-created digital pages, and then create a network of friends linked through each other's pages. Blogs and wikis also are rich sources of information, posted by individuals who wish to use the Internet as their soapbox or simply to exercise their First Amendment rights to free speech. A **blog** is an online journal, usually written in chronological order by an individual. A **wiki** is a collaborative Web site that permits users to edit or add content.

It may not seem fair that total strangers can (and do) look at what you have posted on a social network page, blog, or wiki and use it to judge you. Yet the very public nature of the Internet makes it easy to do. In fact, nearly eight out of 10 employers perform online searches to see what else they can learn about the people who have applied to work for them, according to the business social networking site ExecuNet. Surveys conducted by CareerBuilder.com and the National Association of Colleges and Employers have yielded similar results. More than half the companies surveyed by CareerBuilder.com eliminated a candidate because of information they found posted online. The information included poor communication skills, links to criminal behavior, and lies about qualifications. And it's not limited to just a few social network sites. Employers also use Google to search for job candidates and may even take a look at YouTube. An employer cannot ask questions about a person's social life during an interview, but there is no law prohibiting the discovery of his or her interests from online sources. The bottom line: If you do not want a potential employer to learn more than you want to reveal, remove any content you deem off-limits from all public online sources, or least make your pages private or only available on password-protected sites. Exhibit 2-1 lists a few personal items to consider keeping off the Web.

What online sites contain personal information, photos, or videos that may make a potential employer question your fit with their company? Consider the links to friends' pages and postings as well.

_____

_____

_____

_____

Information to Avoid Posting Online	
Age or birth date	Political affiliation
Race	Sexual orientation
Religion	Social activities and party photos that may be viewed negatively
Unprofessional screen names	Personal correspondence or postings intended only for friends and family

Exhibit 2-1 Information to Avoid Posting Online

> What items from Exhibit 2-1 should you consider removing from online sites that you don't want potential employers or future business colleagues to see?
>
> _____
> _____
> _____
> _____

What, exactly, are potential employers looking for in these online searches? In addition to learning more about your demographics and your social and personal interests, they're looking for signals that you'll be a valuable contributor to their enterprise. According to a survey by ERE Media, companies are looking for a wide range of attributes, as shown in Exhibit 2-2.

Attributes Employers Look for in Online Searches

- Résumé content verification—job skills, employment history, contact information

- Presentation and communication skills

- Integrity, intelligence, good judgment

- Professionalism and club/association affiliations

- Creativity or ability to be innovative

Exhibit 2-2 Attributes Employers Look for in Online Searches

In addition to informal online searches, many employers also rely on independent, third-party background checks to verify résumé claims and to uncover anything that may have been omitted. When such background checks are used, the Fair Credit Reporting Act (FCRA)—which regulates the collection, distribution, and use of consumer credit information—requires the employer to notify the applicant when negative information turns up, along with the name of the company that provided the information. To conduct background checks for certain information, such as driving, felony, or credit history, the applicant's written permission will be required. However, informal searches, such as a Google search, do not fall under the requirements of the FCRA. The issue here for job applicants is that there is usually no opportunity to explain or defend the online information, or to correct it if the content contains material errors.

If you have any concerns about what your background check may reveal, consider paying the nominal fee charged by companies such as CareerScreen, MyBackgroundCheck, and US Search so you can be prepared in case questions arise. Just what might show up? Anything you have been charged with—not just convictions—back to age 18 or 21, in some cases. There is no seven-year statute of limitations on what a background check can reveal; so if you have any drug charges or "minor in possession" charges, they could appear. If you do get questioned about your background by the company, don't lie. Depending on the issue, if you are honest and direct with the company, chances are they won't hold it against you in the hiring process.

Another possibility to consider is subscribing to an online service that will regularly scour the Internet on your behalf to locate information being posted about you. Such services search all social networks, professional review Web sites, blogs, online news sources, and digital media sharing sites, such as YouTube and Flickr, in addition to all publicly available Internet sites. One such company, ReputationDefender.com, can even handle the dirty work of getting the negative or potentially damaging content removed.

Branding Yourself Online

Does the growing use of online resources by recruiters mean you need to erase all digital evidence of your existence from the Internet? Not at all. That may send a negative signal as well. Instead, consider the content on the Internet as *an extension* of your résumé and manage it as your own personal marketing space.

Here are some ways to enhance what others may find when they search. First, clean up any postings you've made to social networking sites such as Facebook, Friendster, and MySpace. Remove any posted interests that would portray you as irresponsible or immature, including both text and photos. Consider paring back your list of friends, especially those whose online postings might contain photos of or content about you that you no longer want the public to see. You may even want to ask friends to remove photos of you they have posted on their sites if you think they could be located.

> Which friends do I need to ask to remove questionable images or comments about me?
> _____
> _____
> _____
> _____

Consider purchasing your own domain name through one of the Internet registrants, such as Network Solutions or Register.com. These sites show up in online searches and may prove valuable in countering any negative content a potential employer finds online. When you buy your own domain name, you can then create and post a Web site with positive content that you control. Think of it as your personal marketing space. As an alternative, create a simple Web site hosted by an Internet service provider that at least lets you control the content posted there.

> Go to NetworkSolutions.com or Register.com and conduct a domain name search for your name. Is it available? How much does it cost? Does this seem like a good investment?
> _____
> _____
> _____
> _____

Do you like to write? Think about starting a blog that you can use to express your views. Blog entries are "signed" by the author (you), so your blog should show up when an online search for your name is performed. Some recruiters are starting to use blog-searching tools such as Technorati, Blogdigger, and Daypop to review blog postings. Just make sure that the topics you discuss on any blog will be viewed favorably by a potential employer.

Join a business-oriented social networking site, such as LinkedIn.com. Started in 2003, this network contains close to 20 million professionals around the world, including executives from all the Fortune 500 companies. Think of it as a gigantic electronic Rolodex file. Corporate recruiters are starting to use this site not only to learn more about current job applicants, but also to find people who haven't applied but might be the right person for a job opening. According to LinkedIn.com cofounder Konstantin Guericke, well over 100,000 recruiters are registered on the site. There may be other networking sites associated with your chosen profession that you could join as well. Doing so can demonstrate that you are serious about joining the ranks of working professionals in your field. If you do join such a site, include keywords in your profile that describe you and will help someone find you when conducting a search. Some examples include the very words you used in your résumé.

> Look at the résumé you created in Chapter 1. What keywords might be used to describe you in an online search?
>
> _____
>
> _____
>
> _____
>
> _____

Online Personal Privacy and Information Security

The use of online searches by corporate recruiters may be disturbing to some applicants, but the fact that an immense amount of personal information can be sourced electronically should not be a surprise to you. The challenge, as you have discovered earlier in the chapter, is managing the information that is available online. By remaining aware of potential uses and risks, employing common sense, and taking precautions, you can maintain a comfortable level of security and privacy. The following section discusses some laws, practices, and tools that can help.

Privacy Laws

Concern about privacy has led to the enactment of federal and state laws regarding the storage and disclosure of personal data, as shown in Exhibit 2-3. There are several common threads connecting these laws. For example:

- Information collected and stored about individuals should be limited to what is necessary to carry out the function of the business or government agency collecting the data.
- Once collected, provisions should be made to restrict data access to only those employees within the organization who need such access to do their jobs.
- Personal information should be released outside the collecting organization only when the individual has agreed to its disclosure.
- When information is collected about an individual, that person should know that the data is being collected and have the chance to determine the accuracy of the data.

It is important to note that although these laws provide legal protection to individuals, if you knowingly post or provide personal information for public display on Web sites such as social networks, such protection may no longer be afforded. Most Web sites now provide policy statements regarding the use of personal information. You should carefully review these statements before providing any personal information to Web sites.

Protecting Your Online Security and Privacy

As noted earlier, it's nearly impossible to keep personal information off the Internet. Instead, your goal should be to manage what is already available so that it cannot be used in ways you never intended. In addition to using available security software and tools on your personal computer, you can also employ smart computing practices, such as limiting what you share online. Exhibit 2-4 outlines a few tips from the Electronic Frontier Foundation (EFF) for helping to maintain your personal privacy online.

Selected U.S. Privacy Laws

DATE	LAW	PURPOSE
2001	Provide Appropriate Tools Required to Intercept and Obstruct Terrorism (PATRIOT) Act (renewed 2006)	Gives law enforcement the right to monitor people's activities, including Web and e-mail activity.
1999	Gramm-Leach-Bliley Act (GLBA), also known as Financial Modernization Act	Protects individuals from unauthorized disclosures of financial information and requires entities to periodically report information disclosure policies to consumers.
1996	National Information Infrastructure Protection Act	Penalizes theft of information across state lines, threats against networks, and computer system trespassing.
1996	Health Insurance Portability and Accountability Act (HIPAA)	Regulates the disclosure of patient health information, requires providers to seek the patient's permission before sharing any medical or health-related information, and provides for the reporting of disclosed information to patients upon request.
1986	Electronic Communications Privacy Act (ECPA)	Provides the same right of privacy protection for the postal delivery service and telephone companies to new forms of electronic communications, such as voice mail, e-mail, and cellular phones.
1984	Computer Fraud and Abuse Act	Outlaws unauthorized access of federal government computers.
1978	Right to Financial Privacy Act	Outlines procedures federal agencies must follow when looking at customer records in banks.
1974	Privacy Act	Prohibits federal agencies from allowing information to be used for a reason other than that for which it was collected.
1974	Family Educational Rights and Privacy Act (FERPA)	Gives students and parents access to school records and limits disclosure of records to unauthorized parties.
1970	Fair Credit Reporting Act (FCRA)	Forbids credit reporting agencies from releasing credit information to unauthorized people and allows consumers to review their own credit records.

Exhibit 2-3 Selected U.S. Privacy Laws

Advice for Protecting Your Online Privacy

Only provide information that is essential.	Many Web sites ask you to complete surveys or register when you make your first purchase. If you intend to visit the site often, providing the bare minimum (required fields) may make using the sites more convenient. If you are unsure of the credibility of a Web site, don't provide any information and stop using the site.
Don't reveal personal information inadvertently.	Your browser can reveal your personal details without your awareness unless you change your browser settings. In the browser's setup, options, or preferences menus, check to see whether your name and e-mail address are visible to the Web sites you visit. If you are not using the e-mail component of your browser, remove your name and e-mail address from the account settings for e-mail.
Mind your digital cookies.	For maximum security, you can change your browser's privacy settings to alert you to, or block all, cookies. Your security software may offer additional ways to manage the information Web sites' cookies seek.
Limit the personal information you post on the Web or share with others who may post it.	Avoid posting your home address, telephone number, e-mail address, or other personal data on any Web site that can be publicly accessed if you don't want others to gain access to it. For job seekers, a limited amount of contact information is required, such as a telephone number or e-mail address. However, there are few instances when other personal identifiers, such as those listed in Exhibit 2-1, are necessary.
Remain cognizant of Web security issues.	Never submit a Social Security number, credit card number, or other financial data over a connection that is not secure. Use encryption if you must provide sensitive information. Never provide your username and password to anyone. With the proliferation of spam and phishing scams online, being vigilant about the types of financial information you reveal can minimize your risk.
Keep your primary e-mail address clean.	Consider setting up separate e-mail addresses to keep communications for your professional and personal lives separate. There are many free e-mail account providers available that make this easy to do. Use the free e-mail account for personal correspondence. If this account becomes overrun with spam or junk messages, you can simply discontinue its use and create a new one.
Read privacy policies and review security seals on Web sites.	Get in the habit of reviewing the privacy policy of the Web sites you visit frequently, especially those that ask you to provide personal information. Check to see if the Web sites back up their privacy policy with a seal program such as TRUSTe and BBBOnLine, which provide a baseline of privacy standards.

Exhibit 2-4 Advice for Protecting Your Online Privacy

Think for a moment about the Web sites where you may have entered personal information. Take a few minutes to read the posted privacy statements provided by each site's owner. What do their privacy policies reveal about how they use your information? If you are not comfortable with what you find, take steps now to remove the personal content.

_____

_____

_____

_____

Cyberstalking

KEY TERMS

cyberstalking
Also known as "sturking,"
a cross between _stalking_
and _lurking_. Refers to
the use of the Internet,
e-mail, or other electronic
communications devices
to stalk or harass another
person.

Corporate recruiters, friends, family, and professional acquaintances are not the only people interested in what you post online. Individuals with less innocent intentions can use the same information sources to commit cyberstalking. **Cyberstalking,** also referred to as "sturking" (a cross between _stalking_ and _lurking_), refers to the use of the Internet, e-mail, or electronic communications devices to stalk another person. Women remain the most likely targets of cyberstalkers, although men and children have also been targets.

In one high-profile case in New Hampshire, a 21-year-old man murdered a 20-year-old woman and then killed himself. For days, the police did not know the motive behind the crime. However, upon confiscating his computer, they discovered he had created two Web sites on which he expressed his loneliness and alternating love and hatred for the woman, who was a former classmate. His online journals revealed how the man had paid Internet search agencies to find the woman's Social Security number and place of employment.

Where do cyberstalkers find their victims? Online gathering places such as social networks, chat rooms, bulletin boards, newsgroups, and online auction sites are all sources. With just a mouse click, a cyberstalker can send e-mail messages to the chosen victim and can even set up time-released messages so the harassment can progress over a period of time. Since cyberstalkers can harass their victims from literally anywhere, it is difficult for law enforcement to identify, locate, and arrest the offenders. All 50 states and the District of Columbia have enacted laws that explicitly cover cyberstalking, and a federal anti-stalking law makes it a crime to transmit any communication containing a threat to injure another person, whether sent via telephone, e-mail, pager, or the Internet. Exhibit 2-5 contains some tips to help minimize your risk of becoming a cyberstalking victim.

After reading this section, how would you rate your risk of being cyberstalked? What steps might you take to reduce this risk?

_____

_____

_____

_____

Cyberstalking Prevention Tips

- Don't share personal information in public spaces anywhere online or give it to strangers, including via e-mail, social networks, or chat rooms.
- Don't use your real name or nickname as a screen name or user ID. Pick one that is gender- and age-neutral, and avoid posting any personal information as part of any online profile.
- Be cautious about meeting online acquaintances in person. If you choose to do so, meet in a public place and take along a friend.
- Check the acceptable use policy for your Internet service provider to determine how it handles cyberstalking and complaints. If it fails to provide a timely and adequate response to your complaints, switch providers.
- If you encounter an online situation that becomes uncomfortable or hostile, log off and go elsewhere online. Contact law enforcement if the situation escalates and you feel threatened in any way.

If You Are Being Cyberstalked...

- If you receive unwanted contact, make it clear to the person that you do not want him or her to contact you again.
- Save all communications as evidence. Do not edit or alter the contents. Keep a file with a list of all contact you have with law enforcement and Internet system administrators as you deal with the problem.
- Unless the communications are needed to help law enforcement catch the harasser, set up a filter to block all unwanted messages.
- If communications persist after you have asked the person to stop contacting you, inform the harasser's Internet service provider (indicated by the domain name after the @ sign). Most providers have written policies and contacts for reporting complaints.
- Contact your local police department and inform them of the situation in as much detail as possible. Provide any documentation you have collected to help them understand the situation.

Exhibit 2-5 Cyberstalking Prevention Tips

Privacy in the Workplace

Once you start a new job, you shouldn't stop managing your personal privacy. Besides using publicly available sources to learn more about you *before* offering you a position, it's quite likely that your employer will monitor you on the job *after* you start working. In a recent survey conducted by the Society for Human Resource Management and CareerJournal.com, results pointed to technology as a great enabler of monitoring. Everything from computer and Internet use to cell phone activity to e-mails comes under the scrutiny of employers. Exhibit 2-6 summarizes some of the key findings from the survey.

There are obvious competitive and proprietary reasons for employers to be concerned about what employees are doing and sharing via technology. But companies also want to protect against hackers, viruses, and other intruders while maintaining a safe working environment. Employees believe employers monitor them to ensure they are productive, not sharing company secrets, and not applying for jobs outside the organization.

It's not just lower-level employees who are monitored, either. In 2007, Starwood CEO Steven Heyer stepped down from his post after the company's board asked him to explain a series of allegedly suggestive e-mail communications between him and a younger female employee. Personal e-mail communications also are at the center of Wal-Mart Senior Vice President Julie Roehm's wrongful termination lawsuit. In these and other cases, sophisticated software can be used to sift through millions of messages in search of keywords and language.

A vast majority of companies have written policies covering workplace privacy issues. A smart employee will be aware of such policies and monitoring activity to avoid the consequences of potentially damaging use.

Employee Privacy & Monitoring Survey Results

Percentage of Human Resources Professionals Who Agree or Somewhat Agree That Their Organizations:

	Have the Right to	Frequently or Occasionally Do
Monitor employee telephone usage	87%	56%
Listen to employee telephone conversations	41%	17%
Monitor cell phone use in the workplace	76%	48%
Monitor camera cell phone use	86%	18%
Track employee computer usage	90%	70%
Monitor employee e-mail use	87%	57%
Read employee e-mails	53%	30%
Examine instant message usage	87%	31%
Track Internet use	91%	72%

Source: "Workplace Privacy Poll Findings," published by the Society for Human Resource Management, January 2005. Used with permission.

Exhibit 2-6 Employee Privacy & Monitoring Survey Results

Have you ever been monitored at work by your employer? What activities were monitored? How did it affect your behavior, if at all?

_____
_____
_____
_____

Wrap-up

Managing your online persona and securing your personal information are two important steps you should take right now. In this chapter, you learned about how employers check the backgrounds of job applicants and how they use this information to make hiring decisions. You also learned about privacy laws, personal identity protection, and security measures that can help minimize your risk of exposure to online predators and identity thieves. Finally, you learned about the kinds of employee monitoring performed by employers. Use this checklist to help ensure the information you present online is accurate and is not used in ways you never intended.

	Checklist—Online Persona & Privacy
❑	Take some time now to visit all the social network sites where you have posted content. Go through each one carefully and remove any content that would give your potential employer the wrong picture of who you are. If nothing else, make your pages private.
❑	Change any screen names or e-mail addresses that don't portray you in a professional way.
❑	Sign up for a new, free e-mail account for your personal correspondence.
❑	Google yourself. Don't stop with just your name—enter your phone numbers, addresses, and any other set of keywords that might be used to find you. Try other search engines as well, such as MSN.com, Dogpile, Ask.com, and Yahoo!.
❑	Sign up for a Google Alert (www.google.com/alerts) if you think your name might end up in the news.
❑	Try to get cached content removed from Google or other sites. Cached content is old information that doesn't immediately appear when Google returns a hit, but can be accessed by clicking on the link to cached content. Check back every few months because they often restore archived content from backups—which means that your "removed" cached content will re-appear without your knowledge. Google posts information about how to do this under Help on its Web site.
❑	Get a free copy of your credit report at www.annualcreditreport.com and check it for accuracy. (Note: This is *not* the same site as the fee-based www.freecreditreport.com.)
❑	Check your browser's security settings to make sure they are set at the level you are most comfortable with.
❑	Investigate your current or potential employer's privacy policies with regard to employee monitoring through a Web search, company human resources policies, or the company's intranet resources.

Tech Skills and Web Resources

Web Resources
Read more about background check information at:
www.collegerecruiter.com/pages/questions/question222.php

For more information on corporate use of social networks:
www.careerbuilder.com

Web sites for business social networks:
www.linkedIn.com
www.spoke.com
www.jigsaw.com
www.ryze.com

Microsoft has good information about protecting your personal information online:
www.microsoft.com/protect/yourself/personal/default.mspx

Projects

Video Briefing

Recruiter Checking Backgrounds of Applicants

In video Episode 1, you watched three student candidates—Matthew, Jill, and Sophie—going through on-campus interviews with Candace Johnson, the recruiter from Encore. The candidates exhibited varying states of preparedness, which you critiqued for use in your own career preparation activities.

Our story picks up here in Episode 2 with Candace coming back to the office to review interview results from a number of colleges. Watch Candace's introduction on the disc that accompanies this text, and then read what happened back at the office in the section below.

Scenario—Encore corporate headquarters, Candace Johnson's office

Candace: "Over the past couple of weeks, I've interviewed dozens of students at several schools in the region. Now, I'm back in the office to determine who will get the call for a second interview here in our office. Some of the candidates were well-prepared, which definitely gives them an advantage. But there's some homework I need to do before we extend offers for visits."

Candace and her assistant, Fermina, begin poring over the interview notes and résumés collected during the recruiting run. Fifteen students were interviewed. Candace does a quick summary of her observations from the first few.

Candace: "Let's review Sophie Aguilar's résumé and interview. Her appearance was the first sign she might not be good fit for our firm. She was slightly disheveled and wore excessive jewelry—although her suit was OK, if a bit bright in color. I wonder if she looked in the mirror before she left the house! Can you imagine what one of our clients would think? She needs to exude professionalism and competence. And wrong as it may seem, she will be judged on her appearance—which will initially affect how much the client will respect her work. She also didn't seem to have done any research or have any idea of the type of work we do."

"Now, as for Matthew Brady, it's clear his mother is controlling his actions. Although I'm supportive of being close to family, he's an adult who now needs to take charge of his own affairs. We've had enough situations involving parents calling Human Resources when they don't think their child has received a fair raise or promotion, or been given a decent job

assignment. In addition, he gave some signals by his answers that he isn't interested in a long-term career with Encore. What did he say? Oh, yes: '*A job like this could be a good place to start for a year or two before I move on to something else.*' With a short-term attitude, he'd not likely pay attention to details or fully engage in the continuing education we require. He *was* dressed well, though, but I suspect that was mom's doing and not his own. We need people who can think and act for themselves."

"Now for Jill Tanner. She made a good first impression on me. Her resume was impeccable, and it was clear from the questions she asked that she had done her homework on Encore. She looked me in the eye and had a good firm handshake, too, which will impress our clients. The only thing we'll need to work on is her definition of professional attire. Although her suit was nice, the skirt was too short and the high-heeled evening wear is definitely a no-no for the work world. We've seen this before, though, with college students. With a little side discussion about professional attire, she should be just fine. I'd like to invite her in for a second interview to meet the rest of our team, so they can provide their evaluation of her as a potential colleague. They trust me to check out the education and work experience qualifications—all the items on the résumé—so they're going to look for personality fit and interests, and whether they could spend an hour in the car with her while driving to the client location. This will be our chance to sell her on Encore as the best place to start her career at the same time. After all, we do much of our work in groups; so if she meets with their approval and she likes what she sees, we could be extending an offer within a couple weeks."

As Candace finishes reviewing the rest of the résumés and interview notes, Fermina hands her the day's mail. She also gives Candace the results of her informal, online checks of each candidate.

Candace: "Here's a nice thank-you note from Sophie. Handwritten, which is fine, and well-written. I also see an e-mail follow-up note from her, asking when her office visit and second interview will be since she's really busy this semester and might not have time if we wait too long. Hmmm…"

"I see I've also received a handwritten thank-you note from Matthew. But it looks like mom's handwriting."

"I don't see anything from Jill, though. That's a bit disappointing, since she was on the right track up to this point. It would have moved her to the top of the candidate second interview list if she had followed up, but the fact that she didn't won't completely kill her chances."

"As for the online search results, it would appear that none of the candidates bothered to clean up their social network pages. It's OK to have a personal life, but I'd rather not see our employees posting pictures of themselves drinking, or scantily clad. If a client saw these images, it might compromise the integrity of the employee and give the client a reason to question his or her judgment in a professional situation. In fact, we had an incident last year with one of our consultants that put us in a sticky situation and we ended up having to terminate her employment. We don't need that headache again!"

After finishing her review, Candace says, "OK, that's what I needed to make my final recommendations for second interviews."

Video Critique Worksheet

As you reflect on Candace Johnson's comments, and what the student candidates did as part of their preparation and follow-up outside the interview setting, take a moment to write a few notes about what you plan to do in the future.

What did Matthew Brady do right? Wrong?

_____

_____

_____

What did Jill Tanner do right? Wrong?

_____

_____

_____

_____

What did Sophie Aguilar do right? Wrong?

_____

_____

_____

_____

Based upon what you've read, what actions do you need to take to prepare yourself?

_____

_____

_____

_____

Cleaning Up Your Online Persona

If you haven't given much thought to your online persona, now is the time to do so. Follow the actions in each question, and record your results in the space provided.

1. Perform a Google search on each of the following and record what the search results reveal:

    a. Full name (including middle name)

    _____

    _____

    b. Nicknames

    _____

    _____

    c. Address (home and school, if different)

    _____

    _____

    d. Phone number (home and cell)

    _____

    _____

2. Take a critical look at your social network page postings. Have an adult relative or non-relative you respect critically evaluate the contents of these postings. Based on what they tell you, what needs to be removed or made private? Are there any typos or grammatical errors that might give the wrong impression?

_____

_____

_____

_____

3. Once you've started work in a full-time professional position, what rules or guidelines do you think your employer might have about the use of technology and social networks? How will this affect your usage?

_____

_____

_____

_____

4. Some people don't think it's fair that employers perform background checks and online searches before making job offers, claiming that a person's private life is their business and not the employer's. What's your position on this issue?

_____

_____

_____

_____

_____

_____

_____

_____

Personal Identity Theft Protection

Identity theft was the leading consumer fraud complaint lodged with the Federal Trade Commission in 2006 with 36% of complaints centering on this crime. So what is identity theft? Basically, it is the theft of a person's identity through stolen identity information. In the most recent survey year, total losses were estimated at $15.6 billion in the United States. The average loss reported by victims was $1,882. In nearly all cases, the victim did not know the thief. The age group that was targeted the most was ages 18 to 29.

For this assignment about identity theft, start by reading more on the topic at the Federal Trade Commission's Web site, www.ftc.gov/idtheft.

1. What does the FTC mean when it directs consumers to "Deter, Detect, and Defend" against identity theft?

_____

_____

_____

_____

_____

_____

_____

2. What types of fraud can be committed with stolen identity information?

_____

_____

_____

_____

_____

_____

_____

3. How can you protect yourself against identity theft? List at least four practical approaches. If you use a social network, such as MySpace and Facebook, include one or two approaches for those environments also.

_____

_____

_____

_____

_____

_____

_____

_____

4. How might you discover that you have been the victim of identity theft?

_____

_____

_____

_____

_____

_____

_____

_____

5. What steps should you take upon discovering that you are a victim of identity theft? List at least three actions to take.

_____

_____

_____

_____

_____

_____

_____

_____

6. List the top three things you learned from this assignment.

_____

_____

_____

_____

_____

_____

_____

_____

7. The FTC provides information on ways to increase community awareness of identity theft. If directed by your instructor, download the materials provided by the FTC and prepare a presentation that could be given to a local community group, club, or organization.

_____

_____

_____

_____

_____

_____

_____

_____

What Do Your Peers Think?

This chapter has provided a lot of information to help you get ready to enter the workforce. You've had a chance to assess your own personal preparedness, but how do your peers stack up? Conduct an informal survey in your residence hall, neighborhood, sports club, or other group to determine your peers' awareness of and concern about their online personas. If you have a video camera, tape their responses to make a "man on the street" news story about this issue. To get you started, answer the questions listed here. Then, ask several people for their responses to see how you compare.

1. Did you know that when you apply for a job, companies might do an online search to see what they can find out about you? What do you think they look for?

   _____

   _____

   _____

   _____

2. Do you have personal information posted online that you'd rather your future employer not see? If so, what type of information is it?

   _____

   _____

   _____

   _____

3. Have you ever falsified information on a job application or enhanced your qualifications in hopes of getting a job? If so, why? Did it make a difference? Were you caught?

   _____

   _____

   _____

   _____

4. Have you ever worked for a company that had rules about social network postings? If so, what did they require?

   _____

   _____

   _____

   _____

5. How do you feel about employers and other strangers conducting such searches without your explicit permission?

   _____

   _____

   _____

   _____

6. What steps have you taken in the past to protect your personal information?

   _____

   _____

   _____

   _____

7. What plans, if any, do you have to remove questionable content from social networks and search engines?

   _____

   _____

   _____

   _____

3 Communication Skills

Introduction

If you are reading this workbook, chances are that—like most students—your career preparation skills need some attention. Would it be fair to say your communication skills could use some polishing? If so, you are not alone. Solid written and oral communication skills rank among the top requirements every company recruiter seeks in potential new employees. Personable and otherwise qualified individuals have lost out on great opportunities because they lacked the requisite communication skills. Not fair, you say? So many careers depend on the ability to effectively communicate ideas, analyses, and solutions to colleagues, clients, and customers. Therefore, companies simply can't risk making a bad hiring decision.

You may have the technical skill of a black belt—but without communication skills, you will forever be relegated to lower ranks. This chapter aims to highlight the communications areas you should examine and teach you to use the technology at your disposal to make whatever changes are needed now—before you make an embarrassing mistake in front of co-workers, clients, or senior company officials.

Objectives

In this chapter, you will:

- Discover what your writing says about you
- Learn about precision and how to avoid common writing mistakes
- Find out which communications methods are best suited to making your point

What Your Writing Says About You

Once you enter the workforce, you will be called upon to use your writing skills nearly every day of your professional life. Nearly two-thirds of salaried employees in professional positions have some writing responsibility. Whether it's a simple e-mail message sent to a group, a memo to provide information on an upcoming event, or a longer project status report or new client proposal, the quality of your writing tells the world how prepared, polished, and confident you are in your ability to effectively communicate.

Recently, the study of writing and communication skills in the workplace has received a great deal of attention. In April 2003, the *National Commission on Writing for America's Families, Schools, and Colleges* reported that writing is often the skill most neglected in schools. It further called for the nation to launch a "writing revolution" that incorporates, among other things, more time spent on writing tasks in and out of the classroom. It also suggested that technology could be brought to bear on the development of writing skills so that when students enter the workforce, they will have confidence and competence.

Half of the corporate recruiters in the study reported that basic communication skills are one of the key items they assess when evaluating job candidates. As noted in Chapter 1, your first contact with a company is often written—your résumé. To companies, solid writing skills are an indicator of success for higher wage professional work and promotion. Without paying attention to writing precision from the start, you may as well tell companies you are not worth hiring because you won't be around long enough to promote. Your writing is really just an extension of who you are and the kind of employee you will be.

Common Written Communication Mistakes

Most written communication errors can be easily avoided yet are often overlooked. Whether you are pressed for time, don't pay attention to detail, or have never learned the basics of good writing in the first place, this section should help you turn your writing into works you can be proud to claim.

Mistake #1: Lack of Planning and Focus

Most recipients of business communications are busy and will only read what is important and relevant to them at that point in time. This means you must be succinct and to the point. To do this, you need a plan. Consider the following:

- Think about your audience. Who will read what you write? What knowledge do they already possess and what attitudes might they have toward your subject?
- Be clear about why you are writing. Are you writing to inform or do you want action to be taken? Do you hope to change a belief or simply state your position?
- Research your topic. Provide all the necessary information that the reader will need to make a decision or take action, if needed. If facts are included, be sure you can substantiate them.
- Don't be afraid to rewrite or revise. If it's an important document, consider having someone else read it so you can determine whether your meaning is clear. At a minimum, read what you have written out loud to determine whether the message and impact come across as you intended.

How often do you take the time to outline your thoughts before writing? What specific items on this list have you neglected that have caused problems in the past?

_____

_____

_____

_____

Mistake #2: Poor Grammar and Spelling

Application software programs such as Word 2007 eliminate all excuses for not checking your spelling and grammar in written communications. Many e-mail programs even provide the ability to check spelling before sending messages. If yours doesn't, draft your message in a word-processing program first, run a spelling and grammar check, and then cut and paste the text into the body of your e-mail message. Keep in mind that spell-checking doesn't catch every error, so be sure to review your work carefully.

When it comes to writing precision, there are a few basic principles to keep in mind that will make your documents more polished. The first set includes grammar. Exhibit 3-1 lists some common principles you can apply to your writing.

Grammar Tips

- Avoid subject and verb disagreement. A pronoun must agree with the word it refers to in person, number, or gender. Examples:
  a. Everyone wanted his or her grades at the end of the exam period.
  b. The faculty is on summer vacation.
  c. The data are conclusive. (*Datum* is the singular form of *data*.)
  d. The alumni of Texas A&M are very loyal to their school.

- Don't switch verb tense within a sentence, paragraph, or written composition. Proper verb tense examples include:
  a. "Tomorrow I will give blood." Incorrect: "Tomorrow I give blood."
  b. "When the client applauded at the end of the presentation, we knew we had won the account." Incorrect: "When the client applauded at the end of the presentation, we know we win the account."

- Use modifiers correctly by placing them as close as possible to the words they modify. When used incorrectly, the meaning of the sentence becomes unclear. Examples:
  a. Incorrect: "The frenzied crowd was brought under control before too much damage could be done by the security forces."
  b. Better: "The frenzied crowd was brought under control by the security forces before too much damage could be done."

- Don't use run-on or incomplete sentences. Examples:
  a. Run-on sentence: "The music selection was good however I didn't like the second act and couldn't understand what the performers were saying because the volume was so loud."
  b. Incomplete sentence: "The boys at the beach club."

- Use adjectives to describe nouns, pronouns, or word groups that act as nouns. Use adverbs (usually ending in –ly) to describe verbs. Examples:
  a. Adjective-noun description: "He has a bad cold."
  b. Adverb-verb description: "He did the job really well." (Not "He did the job real good.")

For more tips, use one of the online references provided at the end of this chapter.

Exhibit 3-1 Grammar Tips

Which grammar principles give you the most trouble when you write?

_____

_____

_____

_____

The second set involves punctuation. Proper placement of commas, periods, apostrophes, and other marks can make a difference in how your sentences are interpreted. A list of some common rules is shown in Exhibit 3-2.

Common Punctuation Rules

- Apostrophes show possession or indicate a contraction. Examples:
  a. Possession (The group's decision is to promote Gretchen.)
  b. Contraction (This isn't the way home. Or It's the best movie of the year!)

- Do not use an apostrophe for:
  a. Plural nouns (DVDs, CDs)
  b. Reference to a time period or numbers (the 1980s, her 20s)
  c. Possessive pronouns (yours, ours, hers, its)

- Colons are used to:
  a. Introduce a list of items or an introduction for an explanation (Have your child bring the following items: flashlight, sleeping bag, insect repellent, and water bottle. Another example: Life Stories: A Journal for Life's Reflections and Memories)
  b. In business letter salutations (Dear Mrs. Robinson:)
  c. Maximize the impact of a word or phrase that follows (There is only one word to describe the event: magnificent.)

- Commas indicate a brief pause in a sentence and are used to join or separate sentence parts. According to the APA, use a comma:
  a. Before "and" in a list or series (Steph, Jorge, and Mustafa drove to the beach.)
  b. To separate a direct quote from the rest of the sentence (I'm in it to win it, the candidate remarked.)
  c. Between two or more adjectives that describe a noun (Please bring a new, unused gift for the toy drive.)
  d. To separate an introductory phrase or word (However, that wasn't all that occurred.)
  e. To separate the complete date from the year (October 12, 2008)
  f. To separate geographic names, such as cities and states (Boston, MA)
  g. To separate clauses that wouldn't change the meaning of a sentence if they were left out (The airport, which is located thirty miles south of town, is conveniently located near the manufacturing plant.)
  h. Between names and titles or degrees (John F. Kennedy, Jr. or Susan Elrod, Ph.D.)
  i. Inside a quotation mark in a sentence ("I'll take another one," replied Juan.)

- Periods are used in certain abbreviations (J.D., Jr., Mrs.) or to end a sentence. If a sentence ends with an abbreviation that ends in a period, no additional period is needed. When a sentence ends with a quote, the period goes inside the quotation mark.

- Semicolons join thoughts that are independent but closely related. (My favorite food is pizza; I eat it at least three times a week.)

Exhibit 3-2 Common Punctuation Rules

> Which of the punctuation rules in Exhibit 3-2 have you broken?
>
> _____
>
> _____
>
> _____
>
> _____

The third set covers capitalization. Capitalization indicates importance. The rules governing this set of principles are shown in Exhibit 3-3.

Capitalization Principles

Be sure to capitalize:

- Full names of companies and government agencies (Apple, Inc., Internal Revenue Service)
- Most brand names (Peanut M&Ms candy, iPod MP3 player)
- The first letter in the first word of a sentence
- The letter "I" (I went to the concert last night.)
- Proper nouns, names, titles, academic degrees (Dr. Gupta teaches Accounting 255 on the Internet.)
- Locations, historical periods (Waimea Canyon, The Ming Dynasty)
- Acronyms (ASAP, RSVP, GMAC)
- Compass points or regions that are part of an official name (Northern Arizona University, "I was born in the Northeast.")
- Titles of books, plays, articles, films, and music (The Bible, Spamalot, The Graduate, Take Five)
- Nouns followed by a number (Gate B24, Area 51)

Exhibit 3-3 Capitalization Principles

Which of the rules in Exhibit 3-3 have you violated in previous written communications?

_____

_____

_____

_____

The last set discusses some of the more commonly misused words in business communications. The words, with their meanings and usage examples, are shown in Exhibit 3-4.

Commonly Misused Terms

Affect To influence or change	**Effect** To cause something to happen
Amount A total such as a sum	**Number** Quantity comprised of discrete items
Appraise Valuation or judgment of worth	**Apprise** To inform or notify
Bad Adjective (not good, below standard, unfit)	**Badly** Adverb ("I feel badly" means you physically have trouble feeling anything when you touch it)
Between Refers to two items	**Among** Refers to more than two items
Can Means you are able to do something	**May** Permission or possibility
Complement Finishes and completes something	**Compliment** Praise
Continual Very often	**Continuous** Without stopping
Envelop To enclose	**Envelope** A container for papers
Except Excludes	**Accept** To take or agree to
Fiscal Relates to revenue in all its forms	**Monetary** Relates specifically to currency
Fewer For items that can be counted	**Less** For quantities that can't be counted
Good Adjective (good luck) or noun (create good will)	**Well** Adverb (going well, feel well) or noun (in a deep well)
Illusion False perception	**Allusion** Indirect reference
In Indicates location	**Into** Indicates motion or direction
Its Indicates possession	**It's** Contraction of "it" and "is"
Like Similar in character to	**As, or such as** Actual example of something
Regardless (not irregardless)	
Semi- Every other period	**Bi-** Occurs twice in a period
Site A particular location, as in Web site	**Cite** To give credit as a source
Stationary Without movement	**Stationery** A type of paper used for written correspondence
Than Used for comparison	**Then** Refers to a time period
That Refers to people or things	**Which** Refers to things
There At a particular physical spot	**Their** Possessive form of "they" **They're** Contraction of "they" and "are"
Who Refers to people doing some action, as in "Ann is the one who the package is addressed to."	**Whom** Refers to some action happening to a person, as in "Ann is the one to whom the package is addressed."
Whose Belongs to whom	**Who's** Contraction of "who" and "is"
Your Possessive form of "you"	**You're** Contraction of "you" and "are"

Exhibit 3-4 Commonly Misused Terms

> Which of the words in Exhibit 3-4 have you misused in the past?
>
> _____
>
> _____
>
> _____
>
> _____

Precision in writing is also important in the workplace because digital documents often live a long time. They are often copied or forwarded to people you don't know and who won't know the circumstances under which you wrote your communication.

> Based on your writing experience to date, what grade would you give yourself for spelling and grammar? Are you satisfied with that grade? If not, what will you do in the future to raise it?
>
> _____
>
> _____
>
> _____
>
> _____

Mistake #3: Wrong Tone or Language

When you write informal communications, you may use abbreviated or incomplete sentences and phrases or slang. You may even choose to use profanity to underscore your point to family or friends. However, in the workplace, you must carefully consider the tone of your written communication so you don't unintentionally offend your readers. Using contractions is considered friendly and is usually acceptable, but it is never, ever acceptable to use offensive language.

As for the level of formality, once again, consider your audience. A friendly tone is usually welcome in the workplace, as is a positive one. For example, read the following sentence:

> "Our customer service representatives are busy and only available between 9 a.m. and 5 p.m. most days, so don't be surprised if we can't answer your call."

How does it compare to this?:

> "Our customer service representatives are ready to take your call between 9 a.m. and 5 p.m. Since our heaviest call volume is between 9 a.m. and 2 p.m., please call after 2 p.m. for faster service."

Here's another example:

> "We can't possibly fit this project into the schedule before next month."

Compared to:

> "We're willing to work with you to help meet your deadline during this busy time of the year."

Do you see the difference? The second sentence in each group conveys the same information as the first one, yet the tone is much more cooperative and friendly.

Reflect on some recent documents or messages you have written. What was the tone? Could it have been misconstrued?

_____

_____

_____

_____

Mistake #4: Using Clichés and Obfuscation

You probably have a sense of what the word _cliché_ means. It is an expression that has become trite and meaningless as a result of its overuse. How about the word _obfuscation_? It means confusion or intentional ambiguity. When you write, your language should be free of obfuscation, buzzwords, and jargon that will weaken your message or make it difficult for your reader to understand your meaning. For example, it is better to say that you will "set an achievable goal" as opposed to "proactively prioritize target thresholds." In addition, using a bigger word when a simpler one will do can sound insincere and pompous. For example, "Our team will use the resources provided…" sounds better than "Our team will utilize the wherewithal and capital assets provided…" Wouldn't you agree? You will impress your reader more by avoiding these mistakes.

Heard any good clichés lately? Good examples can be found at work, in the classroom, in popular music, on television, and even in social settings. Write down some that you believe should be avoided.

_____

_____

_____

_____

Mistake #5: Inappropriate Use of Active or Passive Voice

Using an active voice when you write conveys energy and action. This is the most common way to write in business since it can be used to motivate or stimulate the reader. Active sentences are shorter and have more life. In active sentences, the subject performs the action. For example, you'd say, "Our company is launching a new product…" instead of "A new product is being launched by our company…" for more impact.

Yet in some situations, the passive voice can be effective. The passive voice is softer, diplomatic, and less aggressive. In this case, the subject receives the action. It is often used in situations involving conflict or tension to avoid being too abrupt or blunt. Here's an example: "In national news today, Encore announced that there will be major employee layoffs starting Monday." This is the passive voice. Here's the same sentence in the active voice: "Encore is laying off employees starting Monday." Do you see how this one is more abrupt?

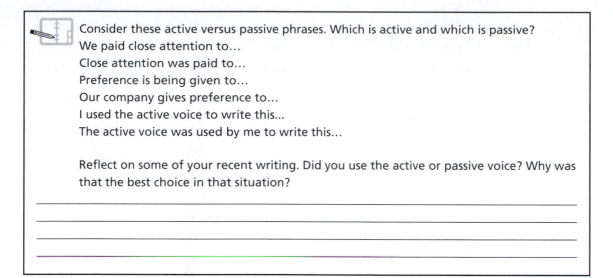

Consider these active versus passive phrases. Which is active and which is passive?

We paid close attention to…

Close attention was paid to…

Preference is being given to…

Our company gives preference to…

I used the active voice to write this…

The active voice was used by me to write this…

Reflect on some of your recent writing. Did you use the active or passive voice? Why was that the best choice in that situation?

_____

_____

_____

_____

Mistake #6: Lack of (Storage) Organization

With so much communication now handled digitally, keeping track of all your files is critical. How many times have you searched for a file on your computer because you didn't properly name it or place it in a folder with related documents? The inability to locate a document or message in a timely manner may cause problems down the road. Known as a **storage hierarchy**, creating folders with meaningful names into which you place all documents related to that topic helps keep your **root directory** (your C: drive) neat and organized.

At a minimum, you should have a folder just for application programs, such as Office 2007. The data and documents related to those programs go into separate folders in My Documents. The name you give to your folders and files can help keep your work organized. A rule to guide the naming of folders and files is called a **naming convention**. Use plain language for the names so that they make sense to you months from now. For example, you might have a folder under My Documents for this semester's coursework. The folder might be named "2008 Fall Semester." Then, in that folder you might set up subfolders for each course so you can keep track of the Word, Excel, and PowerPoint documents associated with each class more efficiently. This is called **nesting**. Your naming convention might be something like lastname_firstinitial_projectkeyword. So, your résumé and an Excel spreadsheet for class might be saved as follows:

> My Documents (on your C: drive, for example)
> C:\2008 Fall Semester
> C:\2008 Fall Semester\CIS 120 Course
> C:\2008 Fall Semester\CIS 120 Course\Slater_B_PersonalBudget.xlsx
> C:\2008 Fall Semester\CIS 120 Course\Slater_B_resume.docx

In the workplace, you can organize your work folders and files in a similar manner. Often, companies provide network storage for work-related documents that gets backed up on a regular basis. Your employer may have standards for file organization and file naming. If so, use those standards to simplify the task of storing and retrieving your work. The same thing goes for your school work now. One more note: try to file as you go so you don't end up with a virtual stack of documents sitting in your root directory.

KEY TERMS

storage hierarchy
A structure that organizes all computer files or folders into a place where all documents related to the same topic are stored.

root directory
The C: drive on your computer.

naming convention
A rule that guides the naming of computer folders and files.

nesting
The process of breaking computer files and folders into subfolders to categorize and keep track of related documents.

> Ask your instructor for the class file naming conventions and preferred storage methods. Is network storage available? How do you access it?
>
> _____
> _____
> _____
> _____

At home, you can mirror the storage hierarchy used at school or work. You will have additional folders and files at home for family members and personal documents. When working with dated correspondence, include the date in the filename to make it easier to sort and locate. For example, a letter written to Mary Bowers on August 24, 2009 might be named "08242009_MBowers." Later, when you go to find it, you can narrow your search by looking for the date. Don't forget to perform regular housekeeping by purging old, obsolete, or unneeded files periodically. This simple task will make it easier to retrieve important files later by minimizing the amount of clutter you have to sift through.

> For personal files at home, what sort of digital storage hierarchy do you need to establish? What naming conventions are needed for folders and documents? What old files do you need to purge that are taking up valuable space?
>
> _____
> _____
> _____
> _____

Making Your Point

Your written communication skills apply not only to memos, summaries, research reports, and proposals. They also carry over to digital communications such as e-mail, text messages, and even telephone use. The same principles described earlier in the chapter for written communications can be applied—although the turnaround time may be much shorter for these digital exchanges. In this case, it makes even more sense to apply a bit of forethought and avoid a hasty, careless response that may create unintended consequences down the road.

E-Mail Etiquette

In today's digital world, many people forgo handwritten correspondence (sometimes referred to as "snail mail") in favor of the speed and convenience of a digital form of communication called electronic mail, or e-mail. In a survey conducted by the UCLA Center for Communication Policy, about 90% of people who use the Internet at work use it to access business e-mail.

Although e-mail is a quick and easy way to send messages, writers should not assume that _anything goes_ with regard to the form, content, and use of electronic communications. In the professional world, what you say, how you say it, and when you respond all carry meaning to the recipient. The informal, abbreviated way you write to friends and family doesn't translate well to the professional realm. In fact, when you send e-mail to people you work with but have never met, they instinctively form impressions and opinions of you based solely upon the quality of your writing. Your friendly, upbeat, and casual attitude when expressed through spelling errors, smiley faces, or inappropriate language can actually backfire to make you look uneducated or worse. At a minimum, you should consider the following items when creating and sending your messages:

- Who is my recipient? If responding to a message with multiple recipients, do I need to "reply all" or just reply to the original sender?
- How quickly does he or she need a response (a lag of several days may be unacceptable)?
- Have I fully answered any questions or provided the information requested?

Exhibit 3-5 provides a checklist of tips that should be part of your professional e-mail etiquette.

Professional E-Mail Etiquette Guidelines

- Don't use all capital letters. This is the equivalent of shouting in written form.
- Refrain from forwarding every joke, cartoon, or touching story you receive. Most people don't have time, especially at work, to deal with them and usually end up deleting them or flagging them as junk mail. This means future legitimate messages from you may be tagged as junk as well. Plus, these messages just take up unnecessary space on the mail server.
- Use proper salutations, such as "Dear Sheri," or "Hello Dr. Bain," or even just the recipient's first name. More informal greetings, such as "Hey, Drama Queen!," are best saved for personal messages.
- Include a meaningful subject line. Something like "Question about Project 2" is more descriptive than "Question."
- Close the message with a simple salutation or your automated signature line. This is especially important when the sender's name is not part of the e-mail address or the system doesn't provide the alias (sender's alternate name) for the recipient.
- Reply promptly, and keep the message short and to the point. Also, avoid the use of excessive punctuation.
- Minimize the use of fancy colors or fonts. Simple, plain text is fine and reduces the possibility of the recipient's mail server not being able to handle the special formatting.
- Avoid the use of text messaging language and abbreviations. Spell out "you" (not "u") and "your" (not "ur"), and use "I" (not "i").
- Only use acronyms if you are sure your recipient knows what they mean.
- Save emoticons for personal communications. Since e-mail can't easily capture the body language or meaning of the sender, they are sometimes used to convey that element. However, they can appear juvenile in the workplace. Instead, focus on making sure that what you write won't be misunderstood based on the language and content you include.
- Don't use profanity. The English language has plenty of rich and meaningful words to help you express yourself without using offensive language.

Exhibit 3-5 Professional E-Mail Etiquette Guidelines

> Which of the tips from Exhibit 3-5 apply to your correspondence? For example, are you guilty of typing in ALL CAPS or sending along every joke that comes your way?
>
> _____
>
> _____
>
> _____
>
> _____

Another important caveat about e-mail communications: they are _not_ private. As noted in Chapter 2, the contents may be stored and viewed by your employer—although few take the time or have the resources to regularly do so. Instead, consider what you write in an e-mail message to be more like a postcard. Contents can be viewed by every digital "hand" it passes through until it reaches the recipient's mailbox on his or her mail server.

Also, remember that e-mail messages are easy to forward—and that, sometimes, recipients "reply all" when they didn't intend to send their comments to the entire mailing list. Bottom line: don't say anything in writing that you might regret later.

Telephone Etiquette

The telephone is an indispensable business technology that makes keeping in touch and doing business both efficient and easy. Whether at the office, in transit, or at home, there is no getting around having to use it to keep in touch with colleagues, make meeting arrangements, or broker business deals. Displaying proper telephone etiquette can be yet another way to set yourself apart as a smart and savvy job seeker or employee. Here are some pointers:

1. Answer the phone after two or three rings with a friendly, business-like greeting. Example: "Hello, Staci Whitman speaking."
2. Smile. Callers can tell, even if they can't see you.
3. If answering the phone for a colleague, take the name of the caller before transfer-ring the call or handing it to the recipient. Example: "May I say who is calling? One moment, please. May I place you on hold?" Then don't leave the caller on hold for more than 30 seconds.
4. If you answer the phone for someone else, there is no need to explain why he or she can't answer the phone. Simply say that your colleague is away from his or her desk or the office.
5. Don't talk with food or gum in your mouth.
6. Speak clearly and slowly.
7. Most phones have voice mail. Make sure your message for incoming calls sounds professional. Example: "Hello, you've reached Tanisha Green. I'm not available to take your call. Please leave your name and number after the tone, and I will return your call as soon as possible."
8. If you will be out of the office for an extended period, change your voice mail mes-sage to give callers instructions on how best to reach you.
9. When making calls, introduce yourself right away so the recipient knows whom they are talking with. Example: "Hello, this is David Albritton calling. Is Professor Chen available?"
10. When leaving a message, speak slowly. Repeat your name and telephone number so that the recipient has time to write it down without replaying the message.

> Think about how you answer the phone. What signal might your current greeting send to a recruiter, colleague, or senior business associate? How does your greeting need to change to convey that you are a serious business professional?
>
> _____
>
> _____
>
> _____
>
> _____

Cellular Phones

Cell phones present a special challenge for businesspeople today. Gartner Group estimates that 1 billion cell phones will be sold globally in 2009. Alexander Graham Bell couldn't have imagined the strong emotions that would become attached to the mobile version of his communication invention. Nearly everyone has a pet peeve about cell phones. A study by the Pew Internet and American Life Project confirms that nearly nine in 10 people say they encounter people using cell phones in annoying ways. The worst offense is having loud conversations in public places.

No one questions the device's ability to provide individuals with complete freedom to connect and communicate with others from virtually any spot on the globe near a cell tower. It's the *behaviors* exhibited by those users that stimulate the ire of the masses, and this irritation shows no signs of slowing down anytime soon. This same study found that more than two-thirds of users say their cell phones would be hard to give up. If this is the case, your knowledge of telephone etiquette must include the guidelines shown in Exhibit 3-6.

KEY TERMS

short message service (SMS)
Text messaging.

> What additional cell phone etiquette rules would you add to the ones described in Exhibit 3-6?
>
> _____
>
> _____
>
> _____
>
> _____

Text Messaging

Short message service (SMS), also known as text messaging, has become an increasingly common way to communicate using cell phones. With phone plans often including unlimited texting, sending short text messages may be an acceptable alternative when it's not possible to take or make a phone call. Adapt the etiquette rules in Exhibit 3-6 to your own text messaging. Remember, it's better to err on the side of courtesy if you want to set yourself apart.

Cell Phone Etiquette

In All Situations:
- Use Caller ID to determine whether to answer a call. If it is urgent or you don't risk offending anyone with your conversation, take the call. If you're with a group of people, excuse yourself before taking the call and step away from the group so they don't have to listen to your conversation or attempt to talk over your voice.
- Use voice mail to leave a brief message if the recipient doesn't answer.
- Don't talk loudly or shout into your phone. If the connection is poor, yelling won't improve the signal strength.
- Avoid using profanity in public, no matter what vocal volume you use.
- Keep calls brief when you are with other people. Doing otherwise implies that the caller is more important than those you are with in person.
- Practice, by touch and without looking, locating the button that will silence your phone in case you forget to turn it off.
- When possible, put a distance of 10 feet or two arms' length from other people when using the phone.
- Select a non-offensive ringtone. Anything else marks you as juvenile.
- Consider removing your Bluetooth earpiece when you are not planning to use it. You are plenty cool without it!
- If you are uncertain about whether to mute or turn off your phone, err on the side of courtesy by turning it off or putting it into vibrate or silent mode.

In the Office:
- Set your cell phone to silent or vibrate mode during meetings. Taking calls during meetings sends the message that the caller is more important than those in the room.
- If you are expecting an important call that may come during a meeting, inform participants at the start that you may need to step out to take a call.
- If you are the one making a presentation, don't stop to answer your phone if it does ring.

In Restaurants:
- Turn off your cell phone or set to vibrate only. If you are expecting a call that you must take, inform your dining partners ahead of time. If the call comes, excuse yourself, leave the table, and go outside or to a location that won't annoy other diners. Make the call as brief as possible.
- With a date or business contact, there are few calls that are more important than the people you are with. If your phone does vibrate, you'll impress them by silencing it, ignoring it, or looking at the Caller ID and stating you will call the person back later.

In Transit:
- If not prohibited by the transit authority or carrier, speak with a normal volume level. Imagine having a conversation with the person next to you; there is no need to shout.
- Observe the laws of your state when driving. The safest choice is to not use the phone at all.

At Social Events, Theatres, or Places of Worship:
- Turn off your cell phone or set to vibrate only if you are expecting an important call, such as from the babysitter.
- If a call comes through that you must take, excuse yourself and go the lobby to take the call.

Exhibit 3-6 Cell Phone Etiquette

Wrap-up

In this chapter, you discovered how poor communication skills can damage your professional life. Your grammar, spelling, vocabulary, and organization all play a role in how you are perceived. Some of the big communication mistakes commonly made by business professionals were presented for your personal evaluation. You also learned about etiquette associated with e-mail, cell phones, and text messaging as it relates to career success.

	Checklist—Grammar & Etiquette
❑	Get in the habit of using the spell-check and grammar features of Word 2007 (Review tab, Proofing group).
❑	To expand your vocabulary, try using the Thesaurus feature in Word 2007 (Review tab, Proofing group).
❑	Consider creating an automated signature line for your e-mail communications. Look in your e-mail program's Help menu or ask your system administrator for guidance.
❑	Revisit the e-mail etiquette section and decide what changes you need to make to your own communication.
❑	Observe the telephone etiquette guidelines provided in Exhibit 3-6.

Tech Skills and Web Resources

Web Resources
A few good Web sites for general background on Internet trends and technology use:
www.pewinternet.org/reports.asp

Good resources for information on grammar:
Abell, Alicia. *Business Grammar, Style, and Usage: The Most Used Desk Reference for Articulate and Polished Business Writing and Speaking by Executives Worldwide*. Boston, MA: Aspatore Books/Thomson, 2003.
Essential Managers: Writing Skills. Adapted from a Brazilian book by José Paulo Moreira de Oliveira and Carlos Alberto Paula Motta. New York: DK Publishing, Inc., 2002.
http://grammar.quickanddirtytips.com/he-they-generic-personal-pronoun.aspx
www.grammarbook.com

A great resource for e-mail etiquette and written communications in general:
http://owl.english.purdue.edu/owl/

Projects

Video Briefing

Of the three students, Jill Tanner was offered a second interview. After coming in for an office visit to meet the rest of Encore's consultants, both Jill and Encore's team members thought she'd be a good fit for the company and they offered her a job.

Jill accepted the position and has started working, along with another new college graduate, Marcus Jordan. One of their first work assignments has come from Encore's managing partner, Catherine Parker. She has heard that many new college graduates are interested in being entrepreneurial, so she's asked them to each prepare a one-page overview of how Encore might create an environment to support that interest. Catherine wants to use the briefings as part of the company's quarterly off-site continuing education program for consultants. Listen in as Jill and Marcus talk to you about how they plan to complete this task.

Jill: "I'm so excited to begin my career at Encore and start using the knowledge I gained in college. One of the groups I hope to be assigned to is the financial services team. But I know I have to first complete Encore's new employee training and orientation program."

Marcus: "The career Encore is offering me is just what I thought I'd be doing when I graduated from college. I majored in computer information systems and want to use my technical background to make a difference for the company's clients. I'm not sure what group I'll be assigned to yet, but I figure that technical skills can be used for just about any industry."

Jill: "As the two newest employees, Marcus and I have each been asked by our managing partner, Catherine Parker, to investigate ways that Encore could foster the entrepreneurial interests of new employees like me. I talked with some of my friends to get some ideas, and they think being their own boss will help them gain the work-life balance they want. My guess is that, since we're not assigned to teams yet, Catherine wants to give us some practice doing research, writing, and making internal presentations before turning us loose on Encore clients."

Marcus: "I want to ensure that my first written assignment doesn't make a bad first impression! I don't know what Jill is going to do. But after I've done my research, I'm going to use a few online writing Web sites I learned about in school to be sure I'm not making any writing mistakes. In my Business Communications class, we practiced writing short reports; but I may also look online to brush up on some tips. I also know there are some tools in Word that I can use to check my work."

Jill: "Catherine didn't specify how she wanted us to submit our executive summaries, but I think an e-mail attachment would be OK. Maybe I should also turn my work into a PDF document and post it to Encore's Intranet Web site. Marcus, what do you think?"

Video Critique Worksheet

Review the e-mail and report materials prepared by Jill and Marcus on the following pages. Using what you've learned in this chapter, analyze, correct, and edit their work. (*Hint:* You may need to completely rewrite some parts!) Next, answer the following questions.

What did Jill Tanner do right? Wrong?

_____

_____

_____

_____

What did Marcus Jordan do right? Wrong?

_____

_____

_____

_____

Based upon what you have read, what actions do you need to take to prepare yourself?

_____

_____

_____

_____

Jill Tanner's E-Mail, with Attachment

E-Mail Message

To...   Catherine.parker@encore.com
Cc...   Jill.tanner@encore.com
Subject: Report Summary

CATHERINE,

Please except the attached summary report on the topic of Entrepreneurship in the workplace. i'm sending you an envelop with a hard copy suitable for printing and distribution, and if you tell me the amount I will use our report stationary to make the copies if you want me to.

i hope your happy with my report. i'll keep you appraised of any changes that might effect what I present later this month.

TTFN - Thanks a bunch!!!! ☺

Jill Tanner, consultant

Attachment

DATE: January 15, 2009
TO: Catherine Parker, Managing Partner, Encore
FROM: Jill Tanner, Consultant
SUBJECT: New College Graduates and Entrepreneurship

OVERVIEW
Today's generation of college graduates are optimistic, confident, and ready to make there mark on the world. They also want "work-life" balance and are willing to buck the trend of traditional career paths to get it.

FINDINGS
According to Ellen Kossek, a Michigan state university professor who studies workplace issues employers work-life balance are among the top three concerns between new college grads. For some, this means starting their own companies, however they often don't think about the long term affect and the fiscal implications.

The BLS reports that nearly 370,000 people aged 16-24 are self employed. By comparison to there baby-boomer parents the amount is around 350,000 entrepreneurs. In part, being able to throw up a Web site overnight masks the lack of sophisticated operational knowledge most of these kids have. They also think it's cool to be able to buy the latest cool gadgets and charge them as expenses of there business just to impress friends. Besides the desire for work-life balance these people want the good life and to be rich and famous and see being their own boss as the fastest way to get it.

What does all this mean for today's corporate workplace? Companies need to find ways to let their newest, younger employees express there creativity and enthusiasm by giving them chances to continuously explore they're ideas and try them in a safe environment.

RECOMMENDATIONS

Encore needs to provide employees with a chance to test out there new ideas. The company should set up a special fund and award competitive grants for anyone who wants to try out an idea. Its in the companies best interest to support these employees as the ideas could help the company grow in new directions that aren't previously thought of. Don't kill the enthusiasm by making employees keep detailed records or make too many status reports 'cause that will just in get in the way of taking the ideas and running with them.

Sources: USA Today, 2007. "Gen Y Makes a Mark" by Sharon Jayson; Business Week, August 9, 2006, "Encouraging Entrepreneurship at Work" by Stacy Perman.

Marcus Jordan's E-Mail, with Attachment

E-Mail Message

To...   catherine.parker@encore.com
From...   marcus.jordan@encore.com
Subject: Entrepreneurship Report

My attached report is ready for your review. I hope it compliments the meeting agenda you have planned for the staff later this month. Please let me know whom should review it before the meeting so I may get there input.

If you think the data is good, I can proceed with making up my presentation outline.

Attachment

Entrepreneurship in the Workplace

What Is Entrepreneurship?

An entrepreneur is someone who organizes and directs a business operation, undertaking the risk of profit for its success or failure (Webster, 1973). Entrepreneurship, then, is the expression of this interest by the individual.

Key Factors for Success

For someone to be a successful entrepreneur, the starting place is a great idea and the means to finance it. From there, the entrepreneur needs to have perseverance and focus. In the workplace, this translates into providing the support and resources for employees to pitch, promote, and operationalize their dreams, as long as those dreams are in harmony with the goals of the organization itself.

When an employee comes to their employer with an idea, there needs to be trust between the two parties. The employee needs to trust that the employer will respect the idea and give it fair consideration; the employer needs to trust that the employee is interested in contributing to the greater good of the company by innovating and making a difference through their proposal.

New college graduates don't necessarily want to be defined by the job they do. So while there IS a job to be done for the organization it doesn't mean that's the only characteristic that they want to be known for. If companies grow because of the creativity and innovation of its workers, then they should be given room to grow their ideas. If this isn't offered, they make take the idea elsewhere, and the company loses both the employee and the potential good idea.

Why its Generating Buzz in Recruiting New Employees

According to a 2005 survey by the Higher Education Research Institute at UCLA, 74.5% of college freshmen believe it is essential or very important to be very well off financially. Only 45% of those respondents said it was essential or very important to develop a meaningful philosophy of life. So company's that offer a rigid and inflexible hierarchy that doesn't recognize creativity or reward innovation is a huge turn-off. The best talent don't want dead-end jobs—they want the fast track!

This current generation of new college graduates also exhibit a strong desire to make a quick difference in their world that means business opportunities must let them see there's meaning in bringing their ideas to fruition. They want to prove their value early on, and get immediate positive feedback.

What Encore Can Do to Foster It

In American society, the desire to define yourself is demonstrated by how much stuff you have. So, in addition to making sure new consultants are highly paid so they can afford to buy big homes and nice cars and clothes, Encore can also give them chances to explore their wild ideas without being squashed by older "been there, done that" attitudes between older employees.

Summary

In summary, its important for Encore to recognize the entrepreneurial spirit of it's younger staff, and to provide opportunities for them to express their ideas accordingly.

Think You Can Do Better? Then *You* Write the Report

Jill and Marcus each attempted to provide Catherine Parker with an overview of workplace entrepreneurship. Can you do a better job of reporting on this recent trend in forward-thinking organizations? Then prepare your own report!

In addition to library and online resources, consider interviewing businesspeople in your area to discover what they think about workplace entrepreneurship. Ask your Career Services office which employers have programs for new employees. Conduct an informal survey of your classmates to find out how important entrepreneurship is to them, and whether this type of endeavor is important to their futures and why. If you are already employed, find out whether your company promotes workplace entrepreneurship.

After conducting your research, prepare a two- to three-page report that uses some of the new or enhanced features of Word 2007, such as:

Headers and footers

Citations

Footnotes

Bibliography

SmartArt graphics

Watermark

Word count

Your instructor may require additional Word 2007 features to be used.

A note on plagiarism: Be sure to acknowledge all sources for your information. By not giving credit for the information you provide, you demonstrate both unethical behavior and disregard for the original owner's intellectual property. In addition to written policies, schools and professors now have numerous automated tools at their disposal—such as Web sites like www.turnitin.com—that help them detect such behavior. The consequences can be dire (failure, expulsion) and are simply not worth the risk. If you are unsure about how to properly cite your sources, ask your instructor for guidance.

Using Microsoft OneNote 2007 to Gather Online Resources

In addition to the popular Word, Excel, and PowerPoint applications, Microsoft Office 2007 comes with a product called OneNote that might change the way you gather resources on your computer. Microsoft calls it an "add-on pack for your brain." Interested in learning more? Then read on…

OneNote 2007 is a note-taking and screen capture application that lets you copy text and images from the Internet, take meeting or class notes, organize scraps of information that don't fit neatly elsewhere, and even share what you have with others. If you are completing the first project on entrepreneurship in the workplace, try using OneNote to help you collect your Web sources—with citations—to make it easier to compile your final draft.

To get started:

1. Locate the Microsoft Office 2007 application program listing on your computer.
2. Click to open OneNote 2007.
3. Embedded on the right side of the application are tabs that provide tutorials on how to use the software program. These should help you get going. Read through the first few to get a sense of what the software can do for you.

Your instructor may specify the items to include in your assignment, such as a screen capture with source, text notes, or other items. If your instructor assigns your OneNote work to be submitted for credit, the software even lets you send your work to Word for editing before submission. Be sure to let your instructor know how useful you found OneNote to be for your class work. View the video tutorial on the accompanying disk for more help with using OneNote 2007.

Refining Your E-Mail Etiquette

What's your preferred method of communication: cell phone calls or text messaging? The current generation of college students certainly prefers the immediacy of such methods for keeping in touch. E-mail also ranks highly, which bodes well for future success at work. In fact, nearly two-thirds of executives prefer e-mail over other forms of communication, according to a survey by OfficeTeam. Yet there is a big difference between a casual message sent to a friend and a reply to the boss regarding an important client at work. If e-mail use is so prevalent in the workplace, it makes sense to learn the rules early to avoid making mistakes later on.

Do a Google Search for e-mail etiquette. Select the Purdue OWL site (http://owl.english.purdue.edu/owl/) and one other to help you gain a better understanding of this important soft skill.

What advice is provided about sending attachments via e-mail?

_____

_____

_____

_____

What is "flaming," and why should it be avoided?

_____

_____

_____

_____

Think about e-mail messages you receive. What new etiquette rules should be added to those you've already discovered?

_____

_____

_____

_____

_____

_____

_____

_____

What did you learn from this assignment? How will your e-mail communications change in the future?

_____

_____

_____

_____

_____

_____

_____

4 Team Dynamics

Introduction

In the video episode from Chapter 1, Encore recruiter Candace Johnson asked Matthew Brady to describe a time he'd been on a team. She wasn't just making conversation. With most work done today in teams, companies want to know what kinds of experiences you've had so they can get a sense of how you will do when you join *their* team. If you are like most of your peers, you have spent much of your spare time as a youth engaged in team activities, so such an interview question should be fairly easy to answer. The teams you joined may have ranged from organized sports and musical groups to theatre troupes and debate or chess teams. Your parents knew those activities wouldn't just fill your free time; they would also prepare you for working with others later in life.

It may not have been obvious back then, but your early exposure to teamwork—the joys of achieving common goals, the frustration of motivating slackers—actually was good preparation for what you'll experience in the workplace. As you read through this chapter's lesson, see how often your own teamwork experience pops into your mind. Those early lessons, plus the information here, might just help you make the perfect contribution when you join a team.

Objectives

In this chapter, you will:

- Learn about teams in the workplace, their characteristics, and the roles you may play
- Learn about generational differences and how they affect workplace teams

Teams in the Workplace

By the time you graduate from college and start working, you likely will have been on more teams than you can count. Everyone on the team probably received a ribbon, trophy, certificate, or something to recognize his or her participation or achievement. In the workplace, the types of teams you will be part of may, or may not, reward their members. But know this: you will work on teams and be expected to do much more than just show up. Unlike school, if you choose not to participate, it won't mean a bad grade. It could result in the loss of a raise, a promotion, or even the job itself.

KEY TERMS

team
A group organized to
work together.

synergy
Team results greater than
what individuals can
produce on their own.

formal team
Organized within the
company as part of its
official structure.

horizontal team
Members who are from
roughly the same level
within an organization.

**cross-functional
team (also known
as a project team,
special-purpose
team, or task force)**
Used to solve a specific
problem within a limited
time frame.

**functional team
(also known as a
vertical team)**
A manager and
subordinate workers from
the same department in
the company's hierarchy
who work together to
accomplish everyday
work tasks.

virtual team
A team whose members
rarely, if ever, meet
in person to work on
assigned tasks.

What Is a Team?

The Web sites of this country's most desirable employers tell potential employees they'll be working on teams from the start. At Google, the Advertising Sales team members "work hard to identify [their] clients' business challenges…" Apple's corporate retail team is "the backbone behind Apple's retail revolution." For KPMG, one of the world's leading professional services organizations, you may be part of a multi-disciplinary team or on a team that is "at the heart of our organization." But what exactly is a team?

The American Heritage Dictionary describes a **team** as a "group organized to work together." More than just people thrown together, teams consist of individuals who have skills, talents, and abilities that complement each other and, when joined, produce **synergy**—results greater than those a single individual could achieve. It is this sense of shared mission and responsibility for results that makes a team successful in its efforts to reach organizational goals.

What teams have you been on in the past? What made them work (or not)?

_____

_____

_____

_____

Types of Teams

In organizations, there are a variety of team types. Some are formal, while others are more informal. Some meet in person; others have members who have never met face-to-face. Depending on the work, the type of teams you work on will vary. Knowing a little bit about each one can help make you a more valued member.

Formal Teams

Formal teams are organized within the company as part of its official structure. These teams can be either horizontal or vertical. A **horizontal team** has members from roughly the same level in the organization. When people on a team come from different functional areas of the company—finance, information systems, sales—we often call that team a **cross-functional team**, **project team**, **special-purpose team**, or **task force** because they usually have a specific problem to solve within a limited time frame. After the problem is solved, the team disbands.

A **vertical team**, sometimes called a **functional team**, has a manager and subordinate workers from the same department in the company's hierarchy. The manager is in charge and directs the workers as they complete their tasks. This type of team has a much longer life because the work is not single-goal oriented. Functional teams work together to accomplish their everyday tasks. Exhibit 4-1 shows how horizontal and vertical teams look within an organization's structure.

Virtual Teams, Global Teams, & Technology

A **virtual team** is one whose members rarely, if ever, meet in person to work on team tasks. Instead, technology makes it possible for members to be geographically distant yet work as if everyone was in the same room. Some common examples of technologies used in virtual teamwork include:

- Corporate networks, such as intranets
- E-mail and voice mail
- File transfer protocol (FTP) Internet sites
- Telephone—both landlines and cellular
- Fax machines
- Teleconferencing—both audio and video
- Groupware and collaboration software tools, such as those found in Office 2007
- Social networks, blogs, and wikis

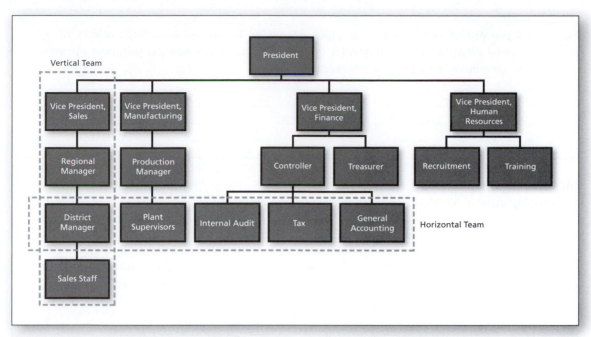

Exhibit 4-1

Virtual teams often must work rapidly to accomplish tasks, so knowing how best to use these technologies is critical. Some virtual teams also have higher turnover because members will join when their expertise is needed and then leave upon completion of their contribution. The leader may change as well, depending on the stage of work the team is completing.

To make virtual teams function well, leaders must spend extra time ensuring that each member is equipped to work together in a virtual environment. This means building trust early, figuring out how best to communicate, and giving individuals a chance to get to know one another. Since the team can't all gather at a local restaurant after work on Thursdays, for example, using technology to help socialize, share photos, and build community can make a difference in team productivity. Effectively using digital communication tools, such as e-mail and text messaging, also can increase team member connection and the ability to get work done efficiently.

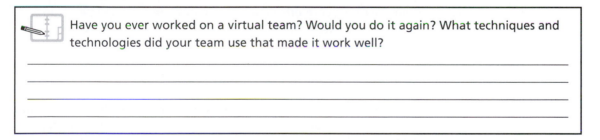

Have you ever worked on a virtual team? Would you do it again? What techniques and technologies did your team use that made it work well?

_____
_____
_____
_____

When team members are across country borders and span the globe, they are often referred to as **global teams**. Many organizations now have presences in different countries. These teams are vital for the organization to achieve its goals at both local and international levels. Global team members bring specialized knowledge to the team related to culture, customs, and language. These team members also help other members understand diversity issues related to goal achievement. If you have studied abroad or are multilingual, your experiences and skills may help you add value to the team's work.

KEY TERMS

global team
Encompasses members who work in different regions or countries.

> If you were asked to be part of a global team, what experiences or skills could you bring? What could you do now (or in the near future) to make yourself more attractive to an employer that has global teams?
>
> _____
> _____
> _____
> _____

Informal Groups

Informal groups sometimes appear in the workplace when the members themselves join forces to solve a problem, work on a task, or simply meet to talk over lunch. Since they are not appointed by management and their duties are not specifically outlined in job descriptions, there is little or no direct accountability or reporting of results to the organization. For example, a group that organizes to clean up the highway stretch outside the office building won't have management directing its efforts. However, the members may get a nice write-up in the employee newsletter for making their workplace environs a nicer place to work.

KEY TERMS

informal group
Groups of people that form without being appointed by management. Little or no accountability or results reporting is expected from the group.

> What informal groups have you participated in? Volunteer work? Social committees? How did those groups compare to formal teams you've been assigned to in class or at work?
>
> _____
> _____
> _____
> _____

Characteristics of Teams

Have you ever heard someone say he is a "team player"? Members on a team get to know how the others work, so they can make contributions where they'll count most. On a football team, not everyone plays the role of quarterback; the team needs other positions working with him if touchdowns are to be scored. However, before the first play is ever made, the members bring their skills to the group and spend time learning each others' moves so they can catch the pass, block, or run toward the goal line together. The best teams have members whose background, skills, and abilities complement each other.

Team Diversity and Size

Team diversity comes in a variety of forms. Gender, race, ethnicity, and age are certainly part of it. But diversity can also be expressed in terms of experience, culture, and personality. A team that is too homogenous may lead to average or mundane solutions. A team that is too diverse may require extra effort just to get everyone heading in the same direction. Yet research concludes that a good mix can lead to greater performance and creativity.

> What experiences with team diversity have you had? How did it affect your team's results? What would you do differently with your next team?
>
> _____
> _____
> _____
> _____

There is no magic number for the size of a team in order for it to function well. However, as a general guideline, a team ranging in size from five to 12 members provides enough diversity for everyone to make a contribution. If there are more than 12 members, subgroups may form, splintering the efforts of the team. Having fewer than five may limit the types of contributions members can make because they may not have the breadth of skills, personalities, or creativity that a diverse team will enjoy.

> Think about your last few team experiences. Was the team size too large, too small, or just right? How did this help or hinder your work?
>
> _____
> _____
> _____
> _____

Roles You Might Play

If a team is to be successful for any length of time, members must see the value in both their contribution and what the team gets out of it. This means two important requirements must be met: task performance and social satisfaction. The job of task performance is usually handled by one or more members who are **task specialists**. Task specialists spend a lot of time and effort ensuring that the team achieves its goals. Often, they are the ones to initiate ideas, give opinions, gather information, sort and cull details, and provide the spark that keeps the team on track.

The **socioemotional role** is handled by individuals who strengthen the team's social bonds. This is often done through encouragement, empathy, conflict resolution, compromise, and tension reduction. Have you ever been on a group that had conflict and someone stepped in to tell a joke or soften the blow of criticism? That person held the socioemotional role.

Both of these roles are important for healthy teamwork. It's like the saying, "All work and no play makes Jack a dull boy." Jack as the task specialist needs the complementary skills of the more social Jill to handle the socioemotional side of things for a healthy balance.

> What roles have you played on teams in the past? If your team lacked these players, how did if affect the team's ability to do its work?
>
> _____
> _____
> _____
> _____

The task specialist and socioemotional roles are important to teams. However, most teams will have other roles as well, including team leaders, work coordinators, idea people, and critics. These roles are not mutually exclusive. For example, the team leader might also be a task specialist, while the idea person also fills the socioemotional role. As your teamwork commences, these positions will be filled—maybe even by you. On a team, no single role is more or less important than the others. The progress and results the team achieves depend on how well the roles mesh in getting the work done.

KEY TERMS

task specialist
A team member who ensures that the team achieves its goals.

socioemotional role
A role assumed by team members who strengthen the team's social bonds.

KEY TERMS

social loafing
Behavior exhibited by
team members who do
not engage in the team's
activities.

Performance Problems

Not every team works smoothly. Sometimes, individuals have their own agendas that run counter to the goals of the team. Others disengage and don't participate at all. This particular problem is called **social loafing**, and is usually the most common human issue teams struggle to overcome. People who are assigned to teams against their will, or who don't have the skill or ability to contribute, may end up "free-riding" on the work of the rest of the team. They get the credit but they didn't do anything to deserve it. Does this sound familiar?

Teams may also suffer from other performance problems, such as:

- Personality conflicts or power struggles
- Different or incompatible work styles
- Lack of clear goals or direction
- Communication breakdowns

What can you do if a performance problem emerges? If the issue is trivial, you can try to ignore it. When it's important to come to a consensus quickly, try working out a compromise, with each party giving a bit. For situations where the outcome is too important and compromise won't work, a collaboration approach—where both parties bargain and negotiate their way to a consensus that lets both win—could be the best solution. Accommodation or giving in for the greater good of the group might work if the problematic parties are both in the wrong and want to resolve the point so the team can move on. Only when a situation is urgent and you need to get your way should you compete against team members to move forward.

On your most recent teams, what performance problems did you encounter? How did you or the team handle them? How do you think managers in the workplace view teams and members who display those behaviors?

_____

_____

_____

_____

Generational Differences and Teams

To better understand why some teams function well and others never seem to hit it off, you need to know something about the people on your team. What do they value? What issues are important to them? Why does it seem that some older (or younger) workers just don't get it?

To answer these questions, you first need to learn a little bit about your generation and how it differs from the ones preceding yours. This aspect of diversity is important to understand if you and your team are going to be successful in completing the tasks you've been given.

Baby Boomers

Generally born between 1946 and 1964, this generation grew up during exciting and turbulent times in the United States. Events such as the Vietnam War, the Kennedy and King assassinations, and the Civil Rights movement and women's movement all profoundly affected the way Baby Boomers think and act today. Space exploration was at its genesis and long-distance travel by airplane became more common as America prospered. This generation had far greater social, educational, and financial opportunities than their parents, which led to higher levels of optimism and personal achievement.

Baby Boomers tend to value individuality, creativity, and individual choice. Many were politically active growing up and maintain this interest today. In the workplace, the homogeneity of previous generations has given way to more racial and gender diversity. Today, this generation engages in activities that promote health and wellness, and is very interested in personal growth and fulfillment, which extends to the workplace.

At work, you'll find Baby Boomers tend to be goal-oriented, with a positive attitude. With the oldest of this generation reaching into their sixties now, they've spent a lot of time on teams. Team-building, collaboration, and group decision making with confidence are hallmarks. They don't like conflict, so seeking a workable solution or negotiating an acceptable outcome for all parties is viewed favorably.

Because Baby Boomers derive much of their sense of self-worth and identity from work, don't expect them all to retire at the traditional age of 65. Medical advances, combined with this generation's commitment to health and need for financial stability, may mean a gradual transition to retirement.

Who do you know that is part of this generation? Your parents, perhaps? How closely do the characteristics listed here match what you've observed?

_____

_____

_____

_____

Gen X

The societal issues that influence this generation, generally born between 1965 and 1982, were tinged more with scandal than ideological conflict. Events such as Three Mile Island, the Iranian hostage crisis, the Clarence Thomas Supreme Court appointment hearing, and the Clinton-Lewinsky scandal all left their marks. Parents of Gen X children divorced more frequently than previous generations.

Television became the babysitter for some of these children, who were called "latchkey kids" because they had parents who were still at work when they came home from school. From this early introduction to independence, Gen Xers learned to be autonomous and self-reliant. They were certainly not coddled or fussed over. Technological innovation really took off during this generation. Computer circuitry shrank dramatically in size and handheld calculators became commonplace. This generation grew up with many new technologies, such as the personal computer and computer games, and is quite comfortable using new devices when they emerge.

The values most frequently associated with this generation include autonomy, pragmatism, and a fondness for irony. There is a strong need to make a contribution and gain both feedback and recognition for it. With a strong independent streak, Gen Xers must work a bit harder on teams but can add great value when they do. Not satisfied with mediocrity, this generation wants to be productive and deliver top-quality results. After watching their parents work long hours and sacrifice time with their families, many Gen Xers vowed to achieve greater work-life balance. They don't "live to work," but rather "work to live" and are proud of it. This attitude can have implications for work teams that may have to put in nights or weekends to meet project deadlines or meet client expectations.

Who do you know that is part of this generation? Maybe older siblings? How closely do the characteristics listed here match what you've observed?

_____

_____

_____

_____

Gen Y

You, like most college students today, are probably part of Gen Y, over 70 million strong. Generally born between 1983 and as late as 2001, parents are most likely to be baby boomers who have indulged them from birth. The self-esteem movement in schools, coupled with a parental view that they are special, has led this generation to be optimistic about future success and even feel somewhat entitled to it. After all, Gen Ys have been praised for doing everything and anything, from just showing up to real achievement against competitive standards. In the workplace, this generation tends to expect reward and recognition frequently.

But not everything has been rosy for this generation. Disasters such as September 11 and the Columbine school massacre have profoundly shaken their foundation and produced a deep-seated need for security. As a result, this generation lives for today and has a short event horizon. The need for immediacy is evident in nearly everything, from communicating with friends via instant messaging or text messages, to doing online schoolwork that auto-grades the submissions and provides near-instantaneous results. This generation has watched previous generations go through corporate downsizings and layoffs, which has given them the sense that work is temporary. As a result, they tend to job-hop and display lower levels of commitment if their employers don't satisfy immediate needs for security and recognition.

Technology, as defined by parents and older generations, really isn't technology at all to Gen Y. Having grown up with, and been given, the latest gadgets and devices to emerge from the research labs, this generation has seamlessly assimilated everything new into their lives with a seemingly insatiable appetite. Learning to use new devices is no big deal, especially if it makes keeping in touch and socializing more fun. With real-time media feeding current events, celebrity news, reality TV shows, and war news constantly to digital devices, this generation is never unplugged for very long. Multitasking when using technology is common and viewed as normal among peers.

This generation is no stranger to teams because they've played on them from their earliest years. The education system has supported them through initiatives for the No Child Left Behind Act, and their peer groups are more likely to be ethnically diverse. With a preference for structure, they are accepting of working in groups and often prefer it to individual task assignments.

Which generation do you belong to? Which characteristics, values, or behaviors best describe you?

_____

_____

_____

_____

As you can see, a little understanding of generational differences can go a long way toward understanding why the people on your team might behave the way they do. But be careful about generalizing regarding attitudes and behaviors. In her book, *Retiring the Generation Gap: How Employees Young & Old Can Find Common Ground*, author and researcher Jennifer Deal found more similarities than differences among the generations. Among her findings: all generations value family first and everyone wants to be respected. She also discovered that most workers want leaders they can trust, and that everyone wants to be trained to do their jobs well and receive timely feedback. Finally, she found that most people don't really like change, especially if there is more to be lost than gained in the process. What this means is that team members must first understand where the others are coming from, which can lead to greater openness, flexibility, and creativity in getting the team's work and goals accomplished.

Exhibit 4-2 contains a simple list of tips to help you and your team members work together better and make the experience a valuable one for everyone, regardless of generation.

Tips for Getting Along on Teams

- Remember that everyone brings something of value to the team.
- Respect and support each other as you work toward the common goal.
- When criticism or questions arise, try to see things from the other person's perspective before taking offense or jumping to conclusions.
- When a team member needs assistance, seek ways to encourage or support him or her so the team's work is not affected.
- Decide early which communication technologies the team will use to keep the flow of information moving smoothly.
- Deal with negative or unproductive attitudes immediately so they don't damage the team's energy and attitude.
- Get outside assistance if team members can't move beyond the obstacle facing them.
- Provide periodic positive encouragement or rewards for contributions.

Exhibit 4-2 Tips for Getting Along on Teams

Which of the tips in Exhibit 4-2 have you tried before with your teams? What was the result? If any of the tips were ignored, how did it affect the team's productivity?

Wrap-up

In this chapter, you learned about teams in the workplace, including the types of teams you may work on and the characteristics of those teams. The different roles team members play were also discussed. You also discovered that the generation to which you belong may play a role in how you approach working on a team.

Checklist—Becoming Part of the Team
❑   Review the types of roles people play on teams to discover which one you are most likely to play.
❑   Evaluate yourself against the characteristics of your generation and determine how they might contribute to your personal success on work teams.

Tech Skills and Web Resources

Tech Skills

Take some time to get acquainted with the collaboration tools found in application software, such as Word 2007, that could help your future teams share and complete work more easily.

Web Resources

Some good Web sites for background on generational trends:
www.valueoptions.com/spotlight_YIW
www.pewinternet.org (search for Gen Y, generational differences)

Projects

Video Briefing

Encore organizes its consultants into teams that work to support each other as they provide services to their clients. Jill and Marcus have been assigned to the same team and have been working at client sites for the past few weeks.

Video Critique Worksheet

Watch the video episode on team dynamics. Then, using the concepts presented in this chapter, critique Jill, Marcus, and their team.

Name	What Generation?	Characteristics Exhibited?	What Team Role(s) Played?
Jill			
Vijay			
Erika			
Marcus			
David			
Catherine			

Of the types of teams presented in this section, which type does the team in the video most resemble?

_____

_____

_____

_____

_____

If you were a part of this team, what contribution might you make and how would it affect the dynamics of the team?

_____

_____

_____

_____

_____

_____

What challenges do you think the team faces (consider type of team, generational differences)?

_____

_____

_____

_____

_____

_____

Teamwork Time

Getting Acquainted with Software Collaboration Tools

As you learned in this chapter, working on teams is not a question of *if*, but *when*. Each team you work on will use hardware (cell phones, laptops, etc.) and software applications that make the most sense for accomplishing work and communicating most efficiently. For example, features in Microsoft Office 2007 make it easier for people to collaborate and share their work with each other. The software enables you to track changes that are made, make comments on what's been written, and much more.

This assignment gives you a chance to learn more about software designed to support collaboration. When your team chooses to use collaboration tools, you'll know what they are and what they can do.

Step 1: Form a group with a few classmates. Have each person choose one of the Microsoft software programs listed below. Research the collaboration tools that come with the software you chose. Then, using Microsoft Word 2007, write a paragraph about the program. Include a few sentences about what the software does, what its benefits are, and how you envision it being used for teamwork.

- Office 2007
- Groove 2007
- SharePoint Server 2007
- Office Live

Step 2: Talk with your team members about your findings. Which product does your team think has the most potential for success? Have the person who researched Microsoft Office 2007 show the other team members how the collaboration tools work in Word 2007 (at a minimum, you should explore the *Comments* and *Tracking* groups under the Review tab in the Ribbon).

Step 3: Send your written paragraph via e-mail to one team member for review and comment in Word (your team will need to decide how to do this). When you get a paragraph from a team member, open the document in Word, turn on *Track Changes* and make a modification to his or her work by adding a sentence, changing a few words, or deleting a line. Add at least two comments. When done, save the marked-up paragraph and return it to the original sender.

Step 4: When you get your original paragraph back with its comments and changes, decide whether to make the suggested changes. For the comments, accept or reject them. Clean up the changes and comments, then save your file.

Step 5: When everyone has completed their e-mail exchange and paragraph revisions, combine all the individual, revised paragraphs into a single document to submit to your instructor.

Role-Play: You're the Producer and Director!

Finish the Script: What Did Jill and Marcus' Team Think?

The video episode for this chapter left off with Jill working to finish the team's presentation. Using what you learned about teams and generations in this chapter, finish the script up to the point where the team makes its presentation at the training meeting. What did Jill do after Marcus left for the day? What did she send to David and Erika? What was their reaction? How did Jill handle their feedback? Where is Vijay during all of this? Did Marcus have anything to say?

When you're done, have your team members role-play the parts you wrote to finish the script. You may even want to videotape your own episode. Do this for each team member's script. Be sure to assume the generational behaviors associated with your character as you act out each role. Which one was the funniest? Most realistic?

Get creative and have some fun imagining how the team managed to get the presentation finished in time for the training meeting.

Encore's Next Training Meeting

Using Word and Excel for Decision Making

With the current quarter's training meeting planned and about to get under way, Catherine Parker wants to start planning the company's big annual meeting. Business has grown and has been profitable, so she's willing to consider taking all consulting staff off-site for the meeting. She has asked all consulting teams to come up with suggestions for where the company should go.

With a team of several students from class, prepare a proposal for Catherine Parker that provides her with the information she needs to make an informed decision about the best location for the meeting. Because many of the Encore teams work with international clients, she wants to see how well several international locations compare to domestic locales so she can choose the best value. As your team selects locations and gathers information (a minimum of two international and two domestic locations), be sure to consider a few of Catherine's other requests:

- Resort locations with leisure activities, including golf and spa
- Good dining options, inside the hotel and surrounding area
- Upscale lodging
- Reasonable ground and air transportation

Your team should prepare an Excel spreadsheet for each location you choose. Each spreadsheet should show the incremental costs associated with travel to and from the location for 40 consultants (transportation, lodging, meals, and leisure activities). For simplicity, assume that the on-site conference costs (meeting rooms and catering) are the same in all locations, so they do not need to be included in your spreadsheet. Your spreadsheet should make it easy for Catherine to compare total costs. For international locations, be sure to convert all currency to U.S. dollars (one Web site to use for this is www.xe.com). As for where the consulting staff will come from, assume the following cities and staff headcounts:

- Five will originate in London
- Ten will originate in Phoenix
- Four will originate in New York City
- Two will originate in Mexico City
- Three will originate in Vancouver
- Six will originate in San Francisco
- Five will originate in Orlando
- Five will originate in Tokyo

A few hints:

- Ask your instructor to designate a set of dates for the annual meeting.
- Document your assumptions about which cities the staff will be coming from to help in determining transportation costs. The Internal Revenue Service (IRS) Web site provides information on meal per diem rates and mileage reimbursements.
- Most cities have a Visitors and Convention Bureau that provides information useful for event planning. Major hotel chains also provide information about their properties and meeting services. If your team thinks a few photos would help sell Catherine on your selections, be sure to include them.

Additionally, Catherine would like an executive summary for each location so she can learn more about what it has to offer. Be sure to address Catherine's requests listed above.

Finally, in your report, provide Catherine with your location recommendation and explain why your team believes it is the best choice for the annual meeting.

5 Presentation Skills

Introduction

We've all been there—witnessing school presentations given by classmates who don't know what they're talking about, or who drone on without any enthusiasm for their topic. We've watched speakers who don't use any visual aids, use too many, or use the wrong kind to make their point. And, we have seen PowerPoint slide shows that are disorganized or look like the work of a kindergartener. Maybe this has even been you. This chapter will introduce you to a simple approach that you can apply to any situation to set yourself apart and make a positive and memorable impression on your audience.

Objectives

In this chapter, you will:

- Learn a simple four-step approach to creating effective presentations
- Find out how to avoid the most common presentation mistakes
- Discover a few pointers you can apply immediately to your next presentation
- Learn basic PowerPoint presentation dos and don'ts

Creating Effective Presentations

The best presentations are planned well in advance of their delivery. The planning process is simple and easy, yet inexperienced presenters often forget some of the steps. No one really wants to be seen as an amateur. Therefore, to prepare for your presentation, you should study the following four-step process:

Step 1: Planning

As you begin preparing for your presentation, you need to ask a few key questions to help you plan what to say. If you can't answer these questions at the start, your presentation will fail to deliver its message or motivate your audience to take any action. Conversely, with clear answers to these simple questions, you'll be better able to focus your attention on providing an organized, logical, and meaningful presentation.

- **What is the purpose of your presentation?**

  In other words, what action or response do you want your audience to have? If it's a sales pitch, you'll want them to buy what you're selling. If you are delivering good or bad news, you'll want them to hear the message clearly and take action based on the facts you provide.

- **Who is your audience?**

Think about their needs and interests as well as the decisions they'll make as a result of what you have to say. Timothy Koegel, author of *The Exceptional Presenter,* states that 90% of what you say will be forgotten within 60 minutes. He also states that—believe it or not—the average adult's "undivided attention span" is 15 to 30 seconds. This means what you choose to say to your audience must be relevant to their needs, interests, and decisions or it will be forgotten. You want to connect with your audience by talking *to* them, not *at* them. This will help you hold their attention and increase the chances that your remarks will be remembered longer.

- **How much time do you have for the presentation?**

Some presenters spend too much time on the introduction and end up having to cut their closing remarks short because they run out of time. This diminishes the effectiveness of the entire presentation and leaves a bad last impression on the audience. As you prepare your presentation, consider the amount of time you have so you can pace yourself as you speak.

- **What kind of output do you require?**

Some presentations are effectively delivered with on-screen visuals. Others require printed support materials because there is too much information to be displayed on the screen, or the presenter wants the audience to have something to take with them to help remember what was said. By asking about the finished product, you'll have a better sense of how your message will be viewed and how often it will be seen (via Web or kiosk replay) or reviewed (via print materials the audience keeps for later).

For your next presentation, consider the following questions: What is the purpose? Who is your audience? How much time do you have? What output is needed?

Step 2: Prepare

Before preparing your presentation, make sure you know your topic. The more you understand your topic, the more relaxed you'll be speaking about it. Your knowledge also will help you answer questions from your audience. This doesn't mean you have to be an expert, but you must be able to correctly pronounce and explain terminology, provide additional information or quantitative data to support your main points, and be able to logically guide your listeners through your presentation from beginning to end.

Once you've done the background research on your topic and feel comfortable that you can explain it to someone who doesn't have your knowledge, it's time to outline what you plan to say. There's a classic presentation maxim that goes like this:

- Tell them what you're going to tell them (this is your opening)
- Tell them (this is your message)
- Tell them what you just told them (this is your closing)

It's a simple but effective way of thinking about how to organize your presentation. As you think about what you want to say, start writing down an outline. Consider your main points first. What logical flow must your points have so your audience will follow you to the conclusion?

Once you've prepared an outline of points in their logical order, think about what you're going to say for each one. Script it out if you have to, then talk it through. Do you have too much to say? If so, start paring it back to the essentials. If you keep it short, simple, and focused, your audience stands a better chance of remembering what you said. You need just enough information to help them understand your point, but not so much that they become overwhelmed with details and facts and lose interest in your message.

Consider the kinds of illustrations, graphics, and audio or video materials you'll need to add further interest or support to what you plan to say. A single image or video clip can go a long way toward making a point and may even help you cut back on the amount of text you need to include.

With an outline formed, you can begin putting your presentation into PowerPoint—if that's the medium you think will be most effective at underscoring what you have to say. (Later in the chapter, the basic dos and don'ts for PowerPoint presentations will be discussed to help you maximize the impact of your presentation.) In some instances, you may not be able to use PowerPoint to make your presentation. In those cases, consider whether flip charts, whiteboards, or overhead transparencies would be more effective in supporting what you have to say.

> Think about an upcoming presentation you have to make. Sketch out the main points of your outline here. What visuals do you think should be included?
>
> _____
> _____
> _____
> _____
> _____
> _____
> _____
> _____

Step 3: Practice

Presenters who think they can stand up and "wing it" in front of a crowd usually reveal this amateur approach the moment they start speaking—by looking down at their notes, rambling off topic, or turning their back on the audience frequently to read from the slides displayed on-screen. Even the most knowledgeable speakers practice their presentations to ensure they know how the topic flows, what the main points are, how much time to spend on each slide, and where to place the emphasis.

Experienced presenters understand that practice may not make them perfect, but it will certainly make them better. For example, Sir Winston Churchill overcame a severe speech impediment to become one of the 20th century's greatest orators and world leaders. He spent considerable time crafting and rehearsing his speeches so they would deliver maximum impact on his listeners.

Think about your own experience with practice. If you play an instrument, your music sounds better the more you rehearse, doesn't it? If you are an athlete, your performance in your sport improves as you spend time in training. The same basic principle applies to your presentations.

As you practice, get passionate, speak with authority, and smile. If you aren't excited about your presentation, how do you think your audience will feel? By projecting your voice with energy, passion, and confidence, your audience will automatically pay more attention to you. Smile and look directly at your audience members and make eye contact. If your message is getting across, they will instinctively affirm what you're saying by returning your gaze, nodding their heads, or smiling. There's something compelling about a confident speaker whose presence commands attention.

> To see how a simple smile affects how you sound, read the paragraph above this box with a serious expression. Then try it again with a smile. Do you hear the difference?
>
> _____
> _____
> _____
> _____

Where you practice isn't that important. You can talk to a mirror, your family, or a group of friends. If you have a video camera, record yourself and then review the video. Sometimes it can be painful to watch video evidence of your performance, but it often reveals the weaknesses you don't want your audience to see and that your friends or family may be unwilling or unable to identify. Whatever you choose to do, the bottom line is this: if you practice, you will improve.

> Think about the best presenters you've ever seen. How passionate were they about their topic? What makes you think so? Would their presentation have been as effective if it had been delivered in a slow monotone voice?
>
> _____
> _____
> _____
> _____
>
> What approaches to practicing do you think you will be comfortable using? If you've used one of these techniques before, what did you learn?
>
> _____
> _____
> _____
> _____

Step 4: Present

You've planned, prepared, and practiced. The only thing left to do is to present! You know *what* you're going to say and *how* you're going to say it. As you make your presentation, relax, smile, and take your time. With a few deep breaths at the start, eye contact with members of your audience, and the knowledge that you have done the work to get to this point, you should do just fine.

Avoiding the Most Common Presentation Mistakes

Think back to your elementary school days when it was time for show and tell. What did most children do? They stood up, rambled a bit, produced a visual aid, and sat back down. In college, the cost of poor presentation skills may be a poor grade or muffled snickers from your classmates as you stumble through your material. That's OK—they probably were not much better when they started out either.

However, now that you're preparing for your career, it's critical that you correct your mistakes and work on your technique because the cost of poor presentation skills will escalate dramatically when you start working. Lack of skill can cost you clients, career advancement, and even your job. Most businesspeople (and even your instructor!) can tell you stories of really bad presentations they've seen or perhaps even given, and the consequences the presenter suffered as a result. To help ensure that presenter isn't you, here are some common mistakes and how to avoid them.

Mistake #1: Splitting Up the Presentation

One common mistake made by teams is splitting up the preparation of the presentation. One person takes the introduction, another takes some of the points in the middle, and someone else works on the ending. When it all gets stitched together, more often than not, it comes off as disjointed and disorganized. That's definitely not the best impression to make.

Another twist on this mistake is to let one person prepare the entire presentation and then dole out speaking parts to the other team members to deliver. Although the presentation may be better organized, the team members who didn't participate in its preparation will often end up reading the points off the slides. Audiences can see right through these types of presentations and will usually discount the credibility of the speakers in this situation. Instead, spend time as a team working through the basic planning and outlining steps so all members understand the message. With a common outline, each member can then take a portion of the outline to enhance while keeping it consistent with the rest of the presentation message.

> What happened the last time you split up your team's presentation preparation in this manner?
>
> _____
> _____
> _____
> _____

Mistake #2: Failing to Dress to Impress

Just as a professional appearance makes a good impression during a job interview, an audience's first impression of a speaker is also based on appearance. Before a single word is spoken, the audience sizes up the way the presenter looks. Does the person look professional and competent? Will he or she be wasting my time with this presentation?

Think about the roles played by actors in your favorite movies. What was your first impression of their characters when you saw them on-screen? Did you form an early impression of them—good or bad—based solely on how they looked? Your audience will do the same for your "performance." If you need to brush up on what to do, refer back to the pointers in Chapter 1.

> Try an experiment this week. Pay close attention to how you judge the new people you meet. How often did you let their appearance affect your interaction with them? Did your initial impression prove accurate? Why or why not?
>
> _____
> _____
> _____
> _____

Mistake #3: Ignoring Body Language

When you communicate with others, how you look and act can overshadow what you say and diminish the power of your message. Research done by Dr. Albert Mehrabian of UCLA found that 55% of what we communicate is non-verbal. Our voices convey 38% of our meaning. The remaining 7% of our message comes from the words we speak.

This means that although the outline of your presentation and the text on your slides play a role in message delivery, it's your voice and body language that make or break the delivery. For example, a nervous laugh can distract a listener by shifting focus to this annoying habit. Avoiding eye contact sends the message that you don't want to connect with your audience or that you can't be trusted. Fidgeting or absently twirling your hair signals nervousness. Slouching connotes laziness, lack of energy, or disinterest. Glancing at your watch tells everyone you'd rather be someplace else.

Even the placement of your hands sends your audience a nonverbal signal. The best position for your hands is to place them comfortably by your side, in a relaxed position. As you talk, it's fine to use hand gestures to help make a point, but be careful about overdoing it. Exhibit 5-1 summarizes what some common hand gestures convey to an audience.

Hand Gestures	Meaning
Hands at sides	Speaker is comfortable and approachable
Open and outstretched hand	To authoritatively dismiss a comment, direct attention to someone or a visual, or make a statement (Example: "Our client isn't interested in that offer.")
Horizontal slicing or flow	Connotes movement or passing of time (Example: "Today is the last day we can offer the discount. Tomorrow, we implement the new pricing plan.")
Hands on hips	Shows defiance or defensiveness, or issuing a challenge (Example: "I don't like the tone of your voice!")
Hands in pockets	Most often conveys over-confidence or nonchalance (Example: "Yeah, I'm the expert and I know it.")
Hands clasped in front or behind	Indicates a passive or inexperienced presenter; can also indicate vulnerability or that the speaker is withholding something from the audience
Hands clasped at chest height	Most common position; variations include fingers touching (think spider legs), hand rubbing, ring-twisting, nervous pen-clicking, which are passive, nervous gestures
Arms crossed on chest	Tells the audience you are not open to discussion or argument
Hands gesturing while speaking	An acceptable means of emphasizing a point (many people "talk" with their hands); should not be overdone
Hands flailing excessively, or hands that are frozen and never move	Usually signals inexperience or nervousness

Exhibit 5-1 Speaker Hand Positions and What They Say to an Audience

> As you watch others present, pay attention to their body language. What mannerisms did they exhibit that were distracting or annoying?
>
> _____
> _____
> _____
> _____

Mistake #4: Lack of Passion, Energy, or Authority

You did the research. You know the material. You may even be speaking from extensive personal experience. But if your voice is timid or too soft, the audience will assume you don't know what you are talking about and will discount the value of your presentation. If you speak in monotone, the audience won't sense your passion and knowledge of the material. However, be careful not to overdo it. Speaking too loudly or using a "know-it-all" tone will quickly turn off an audience and make them stop listening altogether. When an audience member asks a question, be sure to affirm him or her before answering (Example: "That's a great question. What do the rest of you think?" or "Thanks for asking. Here's what my research revealed.") If you relax, smile, and appear confident, your audience will sense your security, triggering a subconscious feeling of ease and comfort with you.

> Think of a recent presentation you heard. How well did the presenter speak? Too soft, too loud, or just right? What did his or her voice convey to you?
>
> _____
> _____
> _____
> _____

Mistake #5: Avoiding Audience Involvement

When you involve your audience in your presentation, they will pay closer attention to what you have to say. When your school instructors engage the class in discussions, do you remember more of what's said? If you participated in the discussion, chances are strong that you retained even more. The same thing goes for presentations.

An easy way to get the audience to participate is to start with a question and invite responses. Stop partway through to discuss a particularly important point. An additional benefit of involving your audience is that you can do a quick check to be sure that your presentation is on-point and relevant to attendees by giving them a chance to talk back and discuss.

> Which type of presentation would you rather attend: one in which you had the chance to participate, or one where you simply sat and listened? Why?
>
> _____
> _____
> _____
> _____

Mistake #6: Using Excessive Non-Words and Fillers

Non-words and fillers are often signs of weakness. Non-words consist of ums, ahs, hms, and other such breaks in speech. Fillers are phrases that don't add any value yet add length to sentences. Both can dilute a speaker's message because they are not essential to the meaning of what's being spoken. At best, they can make you sound unprofessional. At worst, they can distract your audience and make your message incomprehensible. Most people use them occasionally, but in most cases they don't serve any good purpose. Here are a few examples:

- I, um, really, uh, don't know if, ah, I can really, you know, actually do this.
- To be honest with you, we actually can't figure out why the product launch actually failed.
- Like I said, the company's sales revenue, was, I mean, below, uh, expectations.
- Well, I guess we kind of missed our sales target.

> Listen to yourself as you speak to your friends or coworkers this week. What non-words and fillers do you use frequently? If you can't identify any, ask someone to listen to you and point them out. Then, make an effort to banish them from your speech.
>
> _____
> _____
> _____
> _____

When non-words—such as um and uh—are used, the impact of what's being said is diminished. They add no value to communication. Sometimes people use filler words to soften the delivery of bad news or avoid sounding too opinionated—as in "I guess we sort of need to lay off Stephanie and her team," as opposed to "We need to lay off Stephanie and her team." Can you see which one sounds more decisive and direct?

> Rewrite the bulleted examples listed above for greater clarity. Do you see the potential for a more meaningful presentation?
>
> _____
> _____
> _____
> _____

Mistake #7: Arriving Late and Without a Plan B

Most experienced presenters can tell you of a time when their presentation didn't go exactly as planned. For example, the Internet connection went down, the computer wouldn't display properly on the screen, the projector bulb burned out during the presentation, the room was set up incorrectly, handouts didn't get printed...the list goes on. Those same presenters will also tell you that, although such mishaps can be problematic, having a backup plan saved the presentation and their reputations. Often, just arriving at the presentation location early and testing out the technology and resources in the room will be enough to identify whether there will be issues. You'll have time to correct them or enact your Plan B without panicking.

Arriving early also helps you start to build rapport with your audience. By greeting each person as he or she arrives and casually chatting with each one, you'll help to make your audience feel welcome and ease any presentation butterflies you may have.

> For your next presentation, think about what could go wrong. What contingency plans should you make now in case those things happen? If you appear to be in control of the situation, how will that reflect on you as an employee and presenter?
>
> _____
> _____
> _____
> _____

Mistake #8: Unnecessary Handout Distribution

Many speakers provide printed copies of their presentation slides at the beginning of their speeches. Often, this reduces the need for the audience to take notes on each slide as it's presented. Yet what usually happens is that the audience starts to read through the handouts as soon as they are distributed, getting ahead of the speaker. This means they stop listening. As they turn the pages, the rustle of paper causes a distraction. Pretty soon, the speaker has lost control over the impact of the message.

Instead of handing out materials before the presentation, tell your audience that a summary of your presentation points will be distributed at the end of your session. This way, they can write a few notes only if they feel it's necessary, but they won't skip ahead to the end and miss the great information you deliver. On occasion, you may also want to provide a handout specifically designed to support detailed information you plan to discuss during the presentation. Wait and distribute this handout when you get to that point or your audience will immediately start to read it when it's given out, which could throw your presentation off-track.

> Think about your next presentation. What types of handouts are needed, if any?
>
> _____
>
> _____
>
> _____
>
> _____

PowerPoint Dos and Don'ts

If you go to enough meetings at school or work, you'll quickly discover that some people don't like PowerPoint. Yet if you probe a bit deeper, you'll discover that the problem isn't the software; it's the way the presenters use—or more precisely, *abuse*—the tool in the course of delivering their material. So blaming PowerPoint for bad presentations is like trying to blame word processing software for badly written term papers or newspaper articles.

The fact is that PowerPoint, as a presentation software program, is nothing more than a means for organizing a presenter's speech with visual support. A well-organized and planned presentation will be enhanced by the judicious use of PowerPoint's capabilities. But there's no way it can turn a poorly conceived idea into a winning and compelling presentation.

Here is a list of PowerPoint dos and don'ts that you should consider for your future presentations. If the list looks too daunting, remember that following the presentation preparation steps discussed earlier will help you make PowerPoint presentations that are engaging, interesting, and well worth the time your audience will invest in watching and listening to you.

Dos

- **Start with a title slide.**

  Display this slide on the screen before your audience arrives. This will cue them that they are in the right location. Include the title of your presentation and your name on the slide.

- **Use a consistent theme.**

  A slide show that implements different layouts, color schemes, fonts, or mismatched graphical elements will appear confusing, busy, and distracting to an audience. Instead, select one of the many themes available in PowerPoint that will best suit the purpose of your presentation.

- **Include only simple and relevant pictures, charts, and graphics.**

  The most important part of your presentation is what you say, not the graphics. It's important to underscore your words with visual support, but the graphical elements—whether charts, graphics, or photos—should be easy to read and must relate to what you plan to say.

- **Use audio cues sparingly.**

  The best audio signals are those that draw attention to a significant point you want to make. For example, a speech about increasing profit from a new product introduction could use the sound of a cash register's *cha-ching* at the peak of the presentation. However, using the sound repeatedly will get old really fast. If you're in doubt about whether the sound effect will enhance what you have to say, consider leaving it out.

- **Use custom animations sparingly.**

  For example, if you have a slide with multiple bullet points, you can use entrance animations to keep the focus on each point as you discuss it. When a slide pops on screen with all its points revealed, the audience automatically starts to read each one. To do this, they stop listening. So if you want to talk about each point separately, bring them in one at a time as you need them to support what you are saying.

- **Layer complex charts, text, or graphics in small groups.**

  Sometimes there's no getting around a detailed or complex chart to help explain a point. In this case, break the image into small pieces that can be displayed in a layered sequence. Use distinctly different colors to help differentiate the visual elements. This not only helps focus the audience's attention on the part of the image you want to discuss, it keeps them from getting confused as to which section of the image you're referencing when you speak.

- **Use simple fonts in a size large enough to be read from the back of the room.**

  A clean font that's no smaller than size 24 or 28 is usually a good choice for readability. Minimize the mixing of fonts in your presentation so the theme remains clean and consistent.

- **Employ the 7-7 Rule.**

  The 7-7 Rule suggests using no more than seven bullet points per slide, with no more than seven words per bullet. Many presenters use less than this number to keep their slides simple and looking clean.

- **Press the *W* or *B* keys to temporarily clear the screen.**

  When the W key is pressed during a slide show, it brings up a blank white screen. Pressing it a second time restores the slide show. The B key does the same thing, except the screen changes to a blank black background. Pressing it a second time restores the slide show where you left off.

- **Use dark text on a light background.**

  For maximum contrast and readability, a good presentation will use a dark-colored font on a light or white background to make it easy for the audience to quickly read the content. If nothing else, a simple black font on a white background is a safe way to go.

- **Tell a good story.**

  When a presenter stands up and simply delivers the content listed on each PowerPoint slide, many audience members wonder what value the speaker added by simply talking through the points. After all, the audience can read. Instead, get creative! Tell a good story or anecdote that relates to the points on the slide or to the message being delivered. This will help strengthen the message and boost retention of the main points. Who doesn't like a good story?

> Based upon the presentations you've seen and given, what additional PowerPoint dos need to be added to the list?
>
> _____
>
> _____
>
> _____
>
> _____

Don'ts

Nothing diminishes the credibility of a speaker faster than a poorly designed presentation. No matter how smart or knowledgeable you are, the visual impression you give your audience will stay with them longer and more strongly than the words you speak (refer back to the section on body language). One sure way to make a bad impression is to violate the list of PowerPoint dos previously listed. In addition, here are a few don'ts that should be considered for your future presentations. At a minimum, don't:

- **Skip the titles on each slide.**

  Slide titles give the audience a clue as to the focus of the slide's points. If you leave them off, your audience won't be able to follow the logical flow of your presentation.

- **Layer text on top of a busy background graphic.**

  When the background graphic is too bold or busy, it will compete with the text layered on top of it. If you choose to employ a background graphic, tone it down by changing the color boldness or contrast so that it appears faint.

- **Rely solely on the automated spelling and grammar check features.**

  One sure way to reduce your credibility as a presenter is to have typographical errors in your presentation. The embedded spell-check and grammar-check features in PowerPoint don't catch everything. Instead, do an old-fashioned, non-automated read-through of your presentation slides. If you are not confident in your spelling or grammar abilities, have someone you trust check your presentation for you.

- **Overly animate your slides.**

  Overly animated slides are another way to turn off your audience. With too much action on the screen, the viewer will stop listening in order to watch what's happening on the slide. PowerPoint comes equipped with many different slide entrance/exit, transition, and motion paths, yet the vast majority are simply too busy for a professional presentation. It's fine to use a simple entrance animation, such as *Appear*, for individual bullet points, but resist the temptation to show off your animation expertise by using the flashier custom animation options. The last thing you want is for your audience to remember the motion show you gave instead of your presentation's point.

- **Apply strange combinations of colors, themes, fonts, or styles.**

  Spend some time getting acquainted with all of the color, theme, font, and style choices offered by PowerPoint. Then, use only those that will enhance your message and not overpower or diminish what you have to say. When choosing colors, avoid deep, saturated blue hues, such as cobalt blue. The reason is that the normal human eye can't properly process the red and blue wavelengths that constitute this color. Instead of crisp and clear contents, they'll appear fuzzy around the edges. If you've ever noticed how blurry blue holiday lights look, you have experienced this effect.

- **Use numbered lists with contents that aren't in any special sequence.**

  A numbered list implies a sequential order or series of steps to be followed. If the items in your list do not have to be performed in any particular order, then use bullet points instead of numbers to separate them.

- **Display data-intensive charts or graphs.**

  Busy illustrations force the audience to spend time trying to decode what the image is telling them. This means they will stop listening to you while they try to process what's displayed on the screen. If the point of a graphic or chart is to simplify a message to help the viewer get the point quickly, the last thing you want to do is put so much content into the image that it becomes incomprehensible. You can always distribute a handout with the underlying detail for a graph or chart if the audience needs additional content to understand your point.

- **Create too many slides.**

  One common mistake most inexperienced presenters make is creating too many slides to support their presentation. What usually ends up happening is that the presenter runs short on time, so he or she will race through the slides in an effort to finish up. Consequently, important points in the message are skipped, which may end up confusing the audience or lead to a weak and ineffective closing.

- **Put too much text on each slide.**

  Almost as bad as having too many slides is putting too much text on the slides you do show. Instead of following the 7-7 Rule, putting entire sentences or paragraphs on a slide compels the audience to stop listening and to read what's on the screen. If you do intend for the audience to read what's written, such as a quote, then either stop talking so they can focus on reading or read the slide's content verbatim.

Most of the PowerPoint *don'ts* deal with presentations that are cluttered and overdone. As you prepare your presentations, keep in mind that less is more. With *less* visual distraction, your audience will remember *more* of your message—and that's the whole point!

Based upon the presentations you've seen and given, what additional PowerPoint don'ts should be added to the list?

_____

_____

_____

_____

Wrap-up

In this chapter, you discovered a simple four-step approach to planning presentations. You learned the basic presentation skills that you should consider making your own. You also learned how to avoid some of the more common mistakes presenters make. With all the information you've learned in this workbook, you have what you need to set yourself up for success and to make a good impression in the workplace. What better way to set yourself apart and make a meaningful contribution from the start?

Congratulations on finishing the material in *Soft Skills at Work: Technology for Career Success*. As evidence of completion of this course, fill in the certificate (Exhibit 5-2) at the end of this chapter and have your instructor sign it.

Checklist—Creating Your Presentation
❑   Apply the four-step planning approach to your next presentation.
❑   Review your next presentation carefully. Make sure it includes the suggested PowerPoint Dos, but not the Don'ts.

Tech Skills and Web Resources

Tech Skills

Explore the templates in PowerPoint 2007 that you might use in the future.

Create a custom template in PowerPoint 2007 to streamline your personal presentation preparation.

Use your Web search skills to source content for presentations.

Web Resources

If you're interested in more assistance with honing your presentation skills:
www.toastmasters.org
www.microsoft.com/atwork/getworkdone/presentations.mspx

To learn more about emerging technologies:
The Horizon Report, 2008 Edition, a collaboration between The New Media Consortium and the EDUCAUSE Learning Initiative (an EDUCAUSE Program). Available online at www.nmc.org/pdf/2008-Horizon-Report.pdf

A few online resources to help improve your PowerPoint presentations:
http://presentationsoft.about.com/od/powerpointinbusiness/tp/bus_pres_tips.htm
http://presentationsoft.about.com/od/classrooms/tp/student_tips.htm

For free or nominal-fee images to use in your presentation, check out:
www.istockphoto.com (fee-based but loaded with images)
www.flickr.com/creativecommons
www.imageafter.com
www.everystockphoto.com

As with all content created by others, be sure you understand any copyright restrictions before using images pulled from the Web.

Projects

Video Briefing

It's now time for the quarterly training meeting at the Encore offices. Not all of Encore's staff members are present, but most of Jill and Marcus' team has come in for the day. Some are listening in via speakerphone.

Watch the final video episode showing Jill and Marcus giving their presentation for the team at Encore. As you watch, critique their presentation skills using the material from this chapter and the worksheet questions provided here.

Video Critique Worksheet

Evaluate the PowerPoint presentation prepared by Jill and Marcus. What did they do well? What could they improve for next time?

_____

_____

_____

_____

Evaluate Jill and Marcus' business attire. Does it seem appropriate for an internal meeting (i.e., no clients present)? How does their attire compare to that of the other consultants and Catherine Parker?

_____

_____

_____

How well did Jill and Marcus deliver their presentation? What suggestions for improvement would you offer them? Be sure to consider both their presentation skills and the support materials they used.

_____

_____

_____

_____

What do you think about the behavior of the other meeting participants?

_____

_____

_____

_____

Assume you are a new consultant assigned to Jill and Marcus' team. As the newest team member, you are given the responsibility of preparing the team's project update presentation. Using the material in this chapter and the video episode featuring Jill and Marcus, what will you do differently, and why?

_____

_____

_____

_____

Show the Team What You've Got: Rework the Presentation

You've evaluated how well Jill and Marcus did with their presentation to the Encore staff at the training meeting. Perhaps you thought it worked well the way they did it. But you may have seen room for improvement. You might have even decided that you would have taken a completely different path. Using what you know about effective presentations and PowerPoint, use the main points they presented and rework their presentation.

Emerging Technologies Presentation

Choose one of the emerging technologies or trends from the following list or find one on your own (ask your instructor for permission first). Start by researching the topic. Then create a PowerPoint presentation. In your presentation, provide an overview of the technology or trend, what it will affect, the global implications, and why it's an important trend for society, education, and the workplace. Provide examples as needed.

Emerging Technologies and Trends

- Web 2.0 and Web 3.0 (Define first, then explore wikis, blogs, and other resources.)
- Beyond social networks (Go beyond Facebook and MySpace.)
- Web collaboration and content portability (Hint: Examine what Google is doing.)
- Online video creation and usage (Start with YouTube.)
- Mobile broadband and telecommunications technologies (Consider what's happening with new devices, such as the iPhone.)
- Collective intelligence (Wikipedia is just one example.)

Alternatively, pick a Web site from one of the categories above (this means you need to research the category first) and create a presentation that explains what it is, why it's relevant to society today, and how it works.

Sell Your Location to the Encore Staff

Catherine Parker has read through your proposal for the location of the company's next annual meeting. In case your team's location proposal wins out over those submitted by other Encore teams, she'd like your team to pull together a PowerPoint presentation that she could use to unveil the winning location to the entire staff at the next quarterly training meeting.

Using what you've learned in this chapter, create a compelling presentation that's sure to generate excitement among the consultants as they anticipate a few working days away from the office with their colleagues.

Certificate of Completion

Has successfully completed

Soft Skills at Work:
Technology for Career Success

_____
Instructor

_____
Date

Exhibit 5-2 Certificate of Completion

Bibliography

Chapter 1
Career Preparation

Latta, John M. *Professional Success: How to Thrive in the Professional World*. San Carlos, CA: Windrose Press, a division of Orion Group LLC, 2004.

Wolfinger, Anne. *Best Career and Education Web Sites: A Quick Guide to Online Job Search*. Indianapolis, IN: JIST Works, 2007.

Web sites with general information on career preparation:
Career Services @ Virginia Tech. www.career.vt.edu/JOBSEARC/Resumes/purpose.htm.

Doyle, Alison. "Resume and Cover Letter Guide." About.com: Job Searching. http://jobsearch.about.com/od/resumes/a/aa040801a.htm.

Johns Hopkins University Career Management Program. http://hrnt.jhu.edu/cmp/.

Turner, Joe. "Are Video Resumes for You?" QuintCareers.com. www.quintcareers.com/video_resumes.html.

Wall Street Journal Online CareerJournal. http://online.wsj.com/careers.

First impressions:
Adventures in Education. "Interview First Impressions." www.adventuresineducation.org/College/Jobs/Interviews/firstimpressions.cfm.

Ferguson, Cheryl. "A Second Look at First Impressions." About.com: Job Searching. http://jobsearch.about.com/od/interviewsnetworking/a/interviewimpres.htm.

Reitan, Cheryl Riana. "UMD's Sunnafrank Says it Takes Only Minutes to Decide if a Relationship Will Last." University of Minnesota-Duluth, February 4, 2005, www.d.umn.edu/unirel/homepage/05/firstimpressions.html.

Dress for the interview:
Doyle, Alison. "Dressing for Success." About.com: Job Searching. http://jobsearch.about.com/od/interviewsnetworking/a/dressforsuccess.htm.

ExecStyle. "Reference Guide for Women's Interview Dress Etiquette." www.execstyle.com/eBook/Womens_Interview_Dress_Etiquette.pdf.

Hansen, Randall S., Ph.D. "When Job-Hunting: Dress for Success." QuintCareers.com. www.quintcareers.com/dress_for_success.html.

Reasons for not getting the job:
Frye, James. "Why Insiders Get Hired—And You Don't." Ask the Headhunter: The Insider's Edge on Job Search & Hiring. www.asktheheadhunter.com/gv031105.htm.

Minnesota Department of Economic Security. "Creative Job Search." http://labor.idaho.gov/cjs/CJSBOOK/inter5.htm.

Montana Department of Labor & Industry—Workforce Services Division. "Reasons People Don't Get Hired." www.havrejobs.mt.gov/youth/whynothired.asp.

Chapter 2
Your Online Persona

Collins, Judith M. *Investigating Identity Theft: A Guide for Businesses, Law Enforcement, and Victims.* Hoboken, NJ: John Wiley, 2006.

Esen, Evren, "Workplace Privacy Poll Findings: A Study by the Society for Human Resource Management and CareerJournal.com." Alexandria, VA: Society for Human Resource Management, 2005.

Moore, Robert. *Cybercrime: Investigating High-Technology Computer Crime.* Newark, NJ: Anderson Publishing Company, 2005.

Robo, Regina M. "Telephone Manners." Salary.com, **www.salary.com/advice/layouthtmls/advl_display_nocat_Ser83_Par176.html.**

For video briefing—background check information:
LaRose, Yvonne. "Ask the Experts: Employers Use Background Checking Databases." College Recruiter.com: College Career Connector. **www.collegerecruiter.com/pages/questions/question222.php.**

Use of social networks:
Campus Information Technologies and Educational Services, University of Illinois at Urbana-Champaign. "Social Networking." **www.cites.uiuc.edu/security/beyondbasics/socialnetworking.html.**

Dahmer, Shannon. "Survey: recruiters use social networking sites like MySpace to filter job candidates." Indiana Daily Student, December 7, 2006, **www.idsnews.com/news/story.aspx?id=39784&comview=1.**

Dautlich, Marc and Nick Eziefula. "Web 2.0: new internet, new etiquette…new law?" Times Online, October 23, 2007, **http://business.timesonline.co.uk/tol/business/law/article2725636.ece.**

Langfitt, Frank. "Social Networking Technology Boosts Job Recruiting." NPR, November 22, 2006, **www.npr.org/templates/story/story.php?storyId=6522523.**

Schweyer, Allan. "The Power of Weak Ties (in Recruiting)." Inc.com. **www.inc.com/resources/recruiting/articles/20050801/weakties.html.**

Removing cached Google content:
Google.com, Webmaster Help Center. "Prevent or remove cached pages." **www.google.com/support/webmasters/bin/answer.py?answer=35306.**

Google.com, Webmaster Help Center. "How can I prevent my own content from being indexed or remove content from Google's index?" **www.google.com/support/webmasters/bin/answer.py?answer=35301&ctx=sibling.**

Google.com, Webmaster Help Center. "How can I remove my content from the Google index?" **www.google.com/support/webmasters/bin/answer.py?answer=61062&ctx=sibling.**

Protecting personal information online:
Microsoft. "Protect yourself: Beyond the basics." **www.microsoft.com/protect/yourself/personal/default.mspx.**

Chapter 3
Communication Skills

Abell, Alicia. *Business Grammar, Style & Usage: The Most Used Desk Reference for Articulate and Polished Business Writing and Speaking by Executives Worldwide*. Boston, MA: Aspatore Books/Thomson, 2003.

Bean, John C. *Engaging Ideas: The Professor's Guide to Integrating Writing, Critical Thinking, and Active Learning in the Classroom*. San Francisco, CA: Jossey-Bass Publishers, 2001.

Bowers, M. "MGT 350W - Business Communications Handout Packet." Flagstaff, Arizona: Northern Arizona University, The W. A. Franke College of Business, 2007.

Essential Managers: Writing Skills. Adapted from a Brazilian book by José Paulo Moreira de Oliveira and Carlos Alberto Paula Motta. New York: DK Publishing, Inc., 2002.

National Commission on Writing For America's Families, Schools, and Colleges. "Writing: A Ticket to Work… Or a Ticket Out." College Board (College Entrance Examination Board), 2004, **www.writingcommission.org/ prod_downloads/writingcom/writing-ticket-to-work.pdf**.

Shipley, David and Will Schwalbe. "E-mail may be hazardous to your career." Fortune, (May 14, 2007): 24, 26. Also available online at **http://money.cnn.com/magazines/fortune/fortune_archive/2007/05/14/100008719/ index.htm**.

E-mail etiquette and written communications resources:
The Blue Book of Grammar and Punctuation. **www.grammarbook.com**.

The OWL at Purdue. **http://owl.english.purdue.edu/owl/**.

Internet trends and technology use:
Pew/Internet: Pew Internet & American Life Project. **www.pewinternet.org/reports.asp**.

Chapter 4
Team Dynamics

Armour, Stephanie. "Generation Y: They've arrived at work with a new attitude." *USA Today*, **www.usatoday. com/money/workplace/2005-11-06-gen-y_x.htm**.

Aviles, Kitzzy, Bill Phillips, Tim Rosenblatt, and Jessica Vargas. "*If Higher Education Listened to Me…*" EDUCAUSE Review, vol. 40, no. 5 (September-October 2005): 16–29.

Daft, Richard. L. *Management, seventh edition*. Mason, Ohio: Thomson/South-Western, 2005.

Gilburg, Deborah. "Management Techniques for Bringing Out the Best in Generation Y." *CIO*, October 26, 2007, **www.cio.com/article/149053**.

Heller, Robert. *Essential Managers: Managing Teams*, New York: DK Publishing, Inc., 1999.

Hira, N. "You Raised Them, Now Manage Them." *Fortune*, (May 28, 2007): 38–46.

Jones, Gareth R. and Jennifer M George. *Contemporary Management*, 5th ed. New York, NY: McGraw-Hill/ Irwin, 2008.

Nathan, Rebekah (alias for Dr. Cathy Small). *My Freshman Year: What a Professor Learned by Becoming a Student*, Ithaca, NY: Cornell University Press, 2005.

Sacks, Danielle. "Scenes from the Culture Clash." *Fast Company*, Issue 102 (January 2006): 72–77. Also available online at **www.fastcompany.com/magazine/102/culture-clash.html**.

Pryor, J.H., Hurtado, S., Saenz, V.B., Lindholm, J.A., Korn, W.S., & Mahoney, K.M. *The American Freshman: National Norms for Fall 2005*. Los Angeles: Higher Education Research Institute, UCLA, 2005. **http://www.gseis.ucla.edu/heri/publications-brp.php**

Schermerhorn, John R. *Exploring Management in Modules*. Hoboken, NJ: John Wiley & Sons, 2007.

Strauss, W. and Neil Howe. *Millennials Go To College: Strategies for a New Generation on Campus*, Great Falls, VA: LifeCourse Associates, 2003.

Trunk, Penelope. "What Gen Y Really Wants." *Time*, (July 5, 2007) **www.time.com/time/magazine/article/0,9171,1640395,00.html**.

Weimer, Maryellen. *Learner-Centered Teaching: Five Key Changes to Practice*, San Francisco, CA: Jossey-Bass Publishers, 2002.

Chapter 5
Presentation Skills

Bunzel, Tom. *Solving the PowerPoint Predicament: Using Digital Media for Effective Communication (The Addison-Wesley Microsoft Technology Series)*. Indianapolis, IN: Que Publishing, Pearson Education, Inc., 2007.

Koegel, Timothy J. *The Exceptional Presenter: A Proven Formula to Open Up and Own the Room*. Austin, TX: Greenleaf Book Group Press, 2007.

Kosslyn, Stephen M. *Clear and to the Point: 8 Psychological Principles for Compelling PowerPoint Presentations*. New York, NY: Oxford University Press, 2007.

Reynolds, Garr. *Presentation Zen: Simple Ideas on Presentation Design and Delivery*. Berkeley, CA: New Riders Press, 2008.

Presentation pointers:
Russell, Wendy. "9 Tips for Student Presentations." About.com: Presentation Software. **http://presentationsoft.about.com/od/classrooms/tp/student_tips.htm?p=1**.